Cracking the MCAS

Grade 10 Mathematics

The Princeton Review

Cracking the MCAS

Grade 10 Mathematics

by Jeff Rubenstein

Random House, Inc.
New York

www.randomhouse.com/princetonreview

The Independent Education Consultants Association recognizes The Princeton Review as a valuable resource for high school and college students applying to college and graduate school.

Princeton Review Publishing, L.L.C.
2315 Broadway
New York, NY 10024

Copyright 2000 by Princeton Review Publishing, L.L.C.

ISBN 0-375-75588-8

Editor: Karen Lurie
Designer: Evelin Sanchez O'Hara

Manufactured in the United States of America on partially recycled paper.

9 8 7 6 5 4 3 2

Acknowledgments

Thanks to Russell Kahn, Dave Linker, Karen Lurie, and the staff and students of The Princeton Review—as dedicated to student success as any group of people on the planet.

Contents

Part I

Orientation

Chapter 1

Introduction

What is the MCAS?

The MCAS (Massachusetts Comprehensive Assessment System) exams are not designed to make your life miserable, although sometimes it feels as if they might be. They are designed to measure how much of your standard school curriculum you have learned and can put into practice on particular types of problems. The results can then be used to help schools understand which parts of the curriculum are being taught effectively and which parts need improvement.

The MCAS exams are also used as a graduation requirement for students in Massachusetts. Unfortunately, many students are simply not used to solving problems in the way that standardized tests require, and this can make it difficult for them to show exactly how much they know. That's where this book comes in handy. This book will help familiarize you with the test format and content, and give you some problem-solving skills that are geared toward the problems as they appear on the MCAS—specifically for the Grade 10 Math.

Why was the MCAS created?

In the early 1990s, the Commonwealth of Massachusetts passed a law (called the Education Reform Act) that was intended to standardize the curriculum taught in Massachusetts schools, and to insure that students learned what they needed to succeed after graduation. This act contained guidelines that established what should be taught at various grade levels in crucial areas such as mathematics, English, science, and history. Of course, once these standards were put in place, the Commonwealth needed a way to determine whether the various schools were teaching these subjects effectively, and thus the MCAS was born. The scores of all the students at a given school are put together in order to give a picture of how well the school is doing.

If the MCAS was designed to measure schools, then why does my graduation depend on it?

Good question. Regardless of the original intent of the MCAS, the test is one of the requirements for high school graduation. The grade 10 math and language arts MCAS tests are required for graduation for the class of 2003 and beyond. You should check with your school to see exactly which tests are required for you. Why? In recent years many educators have become concerned that students are graduating high school without mastering certain basic skills. One answer to this is to make all students pass a standardized exam such as the MCAS. Is this a good idea? We're not so sure. But, like it or not, it's here.

How does the MCAS differ from other tests such as the SAT?

The most important difference between the MCAS and the SAT is that the MCAS is designed to be aligned with your high school curriculum—that is, it's supposed to measure a set of ideas that you were supposed to learn in school. The SAT and certain other standardized tests are curriculum-independent, so on those tests you may see problems that you've never seen. But on the MCAS, you will see nothing that is absolutely new—the questions will all draw on material you have covered in school in the past few years.

There are a few other differences that will have a significant impact on your test-taking strategy. For instance, you do not lose any points for wrong answers on the MCAS. This means that on the MCAS you should choose an answer for every question, even if you don't have time to look at one or two of them. We'll discuss this in more depth along the way.

If the MCAS tests what I have learned in school, why is it so difficult?

Even if you've studied the material before, you probably haven't studied it in the particular way that it appears on the MCAS. This is like knowing how to play the piano but suddenly being given a piece of music you've never seen before: The first time through it may be rough going, even for an experienced musician. This may not be exactly fair, but there is something you can do about it—prepare for the test.

The MCAS tests material you should have already learned—nothing on it will be new to you.

Who takes the MCAS exams?

Basically, all students in Massachusetts public schools between grades 3 and 8, or in grade 10, have to take MCAS exams in selected subjects. If you're in public school, your parents cannot legally refuse to have you take the tests. Private school and home-schooled students do not have to take the MCAS exams, but they will be allowed to take the tests in the future, if they want to.

What if I have a disability?

For students with disabilities, appropriate testing accommodations (such as smaller testing rooms) are allowed. You should contact your school counselor or the Massachusetts Department of Education if you fall into one of the two groups below.

- Your disabilities are such that the student's Individualized Education Plan (IEP) team determines that you won't be able to take the regular test. In this case, the team develops an alternate assessment, based on your individual needs.

- You have limited English proficiency. You may be exempt from the MCAS exams if you've been in U.S. public schools for three years or less, and you are ineligible for the Spanish-language version of MCAS.

Who Is The Princeton Review and Why Should I Listen to Them?

The Princeton Review is the nation's leading test-preparation and educational services company. Just a few years after we came on the scene our SAT course became the country's largest because of our unique approach to test preparation. Now we're helping students to perform their best on their state assessment tests. If you'd like any more information about our products, feel free to give us a call at 800.2REVIEW, or visit us on the web at www.PrincetonReview.com.

How to Use this Book

This book contains a chapter on general strategies, four chapters of mathematics review and technique, and two practice tests.

We suggest that you begin by taking one of the practice tests in the back; this will give you an initial feel for the format of the test and help you figure out your strengths and weaknesses. Next, read chapter 2 on general test-taking strategies. Then work your way through the technique chapters (chapters 3–6), completing all of the exercises along the way. Then you should retake the first practice test and correct any mistakes you made the first time. Finally, take the second practice test to see your improvement and to help fine-tune your technique.

Note that the information included in this book is the most accurate and available information on the MCAS at the time of writing. The test may undergo minor changes from year to year, so the specifications of your test may not match exactly those that you see in this book. However, it is most likely that your test will be very similar in structure and content to what is presented here.

This book is broken down into three major sections: Orientation (that's what you're in now), Subject Review, and Practice Tests & Explanations. For the bulk of the book, the Subject Review, all the skills that you're going to need to know for the MCAS exam will be broken down into four chapters. Each chapter corresponds to a major skill that will be tested on the exam. Here's the breakdown:

Skill	Chapter
Number Sense	3
Geometry and Measurement	4
Patterns, Relations, and Functions	5
Statistics and Probability	6

How to Practice

As with any skill, such as learning a foreign language or playing a musical instrument, you will probably feel a little silly the first time you try something new. But with some helpful instruction and some concentrated practice, you can improve. Just remember:

- It's important to set aside some time when you're able to concentrate. Don't try to study when there are a lot of distractions.

- Learn from your mistakes. Whenever you get a wrong answer, review the problem carefully to see what you could have done to get it right.

- It's often easier to study with someone else. Find a friend, parent, or someone else who can work with you; each person will often have different skills that he or she can teach you.

How often should you practice?

The most effective plan is to spend 20–30 minutes of quality time per day. Spend that time working on a single concept (such as theories of economics). You should do this over a period of at least 3–4 weeks. Don't think that you can learn it all the night before the test—it's just not that kind of test. If you only have a week or two before the test, however, we recommend at least an hour of review per night (and maybe more).

For More Practice

To improve your score on the MCAS, there is nothing better than to spend time working on actual MCAS problems. You can find old copies of the MCAS mathematics exams on the website of the Massachusetts Department of Education. Point your Internet browser to www.doe.mass.edu, and you can download or print out old tests for practice.

Chapter 2

Test Structure and Strategies

The Format of the Grade 10 MCAS Mathematics Exam

The mathematics portion of the MCAS exam is given in three testing sessions. Each of these sessions is designed to last 45 minutes, but you are allowed time, within reason, to finish your work. This means that you won't be ordered to stop after 45 minutes, but sooner or later you'll have to finish up because you'll have to move on to the rest of your school day.

Each section of the test will have some combination of multiple-choice, short-answer, and open-response questions. Combined, the three types of questions will comprise a total of 42 scored questions on the entire exam. Let's check out each of these question types to see how they look.

Question types

You'll see three different question types on the MCAS: Multiple-choice, short-answer, and open-response. Here's a look at each type.

> There are three types of MCAS questions: multiple-choice, short-answer, and open-response.

Multiple-choice questions

Most (about 32 questions) of the scored questions on this test will be multiple-choice. You will be given a question and a set of four answer choices. Your job is to find the best answer from the choices you are given. Here's an example:

In an 8-pound bag of trail mix, there are 3 pounds of raisins. If this sample is accurate, approximately how many pounds of raisins would you expect to find in 135 pounds of trail mix?

A. 24 pounds

B. 35 pounds

C. 45 pounds

D. 50 pounds

(Don't worry about this question now, we'll talk about how to solve this kind of problem in chapter 6).

You get 1 point for every multiple-choice question you answer correctly.

Most of the MCAS questions are multiple-choice.

Short-answer questions

About four or five of the scored questions you will see on the test (over the three sessions) will be short-answer questions. On these questions, you are not asked to pick one choice out of four. Instead, you are asked to figure out the numerical answer to a problem and write it in the box that follows the question. Here is an example of a short-answer question:

Gumballs Sold

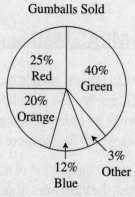

The chart above shows the percentage of each color gumball sold during a certain month. If there were 350 gumballs sold that month, how many would you expect to be green?

In this case, you need to figure out the actual numerical value of the answer and write it in the box in your answer booklet. You get 1 point for every short-answer question you answer correctly.

Open-response questions

Approximately six questions on your test (two for each testing session) will be open-response questions. On these questions, you are evaluated not only on whether you get the correct answer but also on *how* you get the answer. You need to show your work and convince the grader that you solved the problem correctly.

Unlike the multiple-choice and short-answer questions, you can get up to 4 points on these open-response questions, depending on whether you get the right answer and use a correct method. You will get 4 points if you get the correct answer and show the correct work. If you miss some of the answers or don't show correct work, you can get some partial credit. In fact, if you show that you understood the problem, but you got the wrong answer, you can get some points. This makes it very important that you *show your work* on these questions. The way you arrived at the answer is more important than the answer itself.

Here is an example of an open-response question:

> The price of a rare coin was $120 in 1990. Each year from 1990 to 1998, the price of the coin was increased by 5 percent over the price from the previous year.
>
> a. What was the price of the coin in 1991? Show how you found your answer.
>
> b. What was the price of the coin in 1994? Show how you found your answer.
>
> c. What is the earliest year in which the price of the coin was at least $\frac{1}{3}$ greater than in 1990? Show how you found your answer.

Weird testing stuff

There will be a few questions (about five multiple-choice, one short-answer, and one open-response question) on your test, in addition to the regular 42 problems, that will not count toward your score; the test writers want to see how many students get them right in order to decide whether to use them on future exams. These problems are called matrix items. Unfortunately, you can't tell which questions these are, so you have to do them all anyway. But if one or two questions are particularly frustrating, just remember that they might not count. Take your best guess and move on to the next problem.

Here's the breakdown:

Skill	Chapter	# of Questions on the 2000 MCAS exam
Number Sense	3	9
Geometry and Measurement	4	12
Patterns, Relations, and Functions	5	12
Statistics and Probability	6	9
TOTAL:		42 questions

+ about 7 extra (matrix) questions

49 questions

Calculators

You will be allowed to use a calculator for two of the three testing sessions, and you should take advantage of it when you can. Just remember the following rule:

> Calculators can only calculate; they can't think. You need to figure out how to solve the problem before you can begin calculating.

Calculators are great for helping you avoid silly mistakes in your arithmetic, and you should use them when you can. They can help ensure that you make correct calculations, but they can't tell you which calculations are the right ones to make. So be sure you figure out *how to solve* the problem before you start punching numbers into your calculator.

What kind of calculator should you have? You don't need a very advanced calculator, but one with a square root key (square root sign), a fraction key (which should look like $a\frac{b}{c}$), and the basic trigonometric functions (*sin*, *cos*, and *tan*) is ideal. If you do not have a calculator, one should be provided for you; however, you will be much better off if you bring a calculator with which you are familiar. You can find calculators with all of the above functions at any office supply store for less than $15.

> You have to understand how to solve a problem before you can use your calculator.

> Bring your own calculator! Don't rely on one with which you're not familiar.

Formula Sheet

You will be given a formula sheet to use during your test that contains the formulas for area and perimeter of quadrilaterals, the area and circumference of a circle, as well as formulas to convert standard and metric units. This sheet also contains a reference table for trigonometric functions, but you will probably find it easier to calculate sine, cosine, and tangents using your calculator. You'll find an example of the formula sheet in the back of this book.

Scoring

To compute your MCAS exam score, the number of points you received on the test is added. For each correct answer on a multiple-choice or short-answer question, you get 1 point. For each open-response question you can get between 0 and 4 points. Since there will be a total of about 36 multiple-choice and short-answer questions that count toward your score, and a total of 6 open-response questions that count toward your score, you can get a total of about 60 points on the test. (Don't forget that there will be about seven additional questions on your test that won't count toward your score.) The number of points you get out of 60 will then be converted to a standard scale between 200 and 280. Why? So tests with different numbers of questions can all be reported on the same scale.

> Your MCAS score will not figure into college admissions.

Depending on your score based on this 200–280 scale, you will be given a mark of Failing, Needs Improvement, Proficient, or Advanced. The exact conversion from raw to scaled score will change slightly from year to year, but a passing grade requires that you get almost 50 percent of the total points, and a "proficient" mark requires that you get almost 60 percent of the total points on the test.

The following shows approximately how many points you'll need to achieve the various score levels on the Grade 10 Math MCAS exam:

Level	Total Raw Score Points	Scaled Score
Advanced	44–60	260–280
Proficient	34–43	240–259
Needs Improvement	24–33	220–239
Failing	0–23	200–219

By the way, your MCAS score is held only temporarily, for about five years, and then destroyed. Nobody outside of the public school system will see it, so it will not figure into any college admissions decisions.

Pacing

Remember that this test is technically "untimed," which means you should be able to get through most of the problems in the three sessions of 45 minutes. There's no nasty proctor to make you put your pencils down and close the book at the exact second the clock runs out. However, you will have other things to do in your day, and you'll have to stop within a reasonable amount of time, so it is important to manage your time well.

The Two-Pass System

It's important that you don't let yourself get bogged down on any one question. Some questions will be easier for you than others, and if you come up against a hard question, you don't want to waste too much time on it. The best way to accomplish this is to do the questions in two passes.

Here's how the Two-Pass System works: First, go through the test and do just the multiple-choice and short-answer problems you know you can do fairly easily—that's your *first pass*. Then, go to the open-response questions. These account for a large number of points, so you want to be sure to spend a good deal of time on them.

Once you're through with the open-response questions, go back for a *second pass* and try the harder multiple-choice and short-answer questions that you haven't done yet. Even if you can't get the right answer on a harder multiple-choice question, try to narrow down your choices and take a good guess. And don't forget: It's important to guess on every single multiple-choice problem. *There is no penalty for wrong answers,* so you can only gain points by guessing. We're about to show you how.

> There is no guessing penalty, so you can guess on any multiple-choice question!

Get the lay of the land

At the beginning of each section, it's a good idea to take a quick glance through your booklet and see how many problems you have, and what kind of problems they are. Some sections may have several short-answer questions, while others have none. Why is this important? You should have enough time to finish, but if you do happen to find yourself running out of time, concentrate your time where it counts: make sure you have good responses to the open-response questions and good guesses on the multiple-choice questions. If you're running out of time, skip the short-answer questions since there's no good way to guess at them. But a few good guesses on multiple-choice questions, or a few added details on an open-response question may turn into 1 or 2 extra points.

Guessing

You might be afraid to take a guess when you aren't sure of the correct answer, but you must fight this fear on the MCAS exam. Even if you have no idea how to solve a multiple-choice problem or don't have time to solve it, you've got a one in four chance of getting it right. If you don't guess, you're giving away free points. Make sure that you fill in an answer for every multiple-choice question. And if you have time to read the problem carefully, you can probably take an educated guess, which will improve your chances of guessing correctly.

> If you don't guess on the tough multiple-choice problems, you're giving away free points!

On the open-response questions, remember this: You can get from 0–4 points on these questions, so even if you're not sure of what you're doing, write down *something*. Try to reword the question as an "entrance" to an answer. You can probably get a point or two of partial credit, even if you don't get the right answer.

Process of Elimination (POE)

One of the most powerful test-taking skills you can use to score well on standardized tests is Process of Elimination (POE). Sometimes the best way to solve a problem is to figure out what the three wrong answers are and eliminate them. Whatever choice is left is the answer you should pick.

Why is POE a good idea? Because it's often easier to identify the *wrong* answers than to find the *correct* one. Even if you can't cross off all three wrong answers, you can often cross off one or two and take an educated guess from among the remaining choices.

Try the following problem (don't worry, there's no geography on the MCAS math test):

What is the capital of Malawi?

A. Washington

B. Paris

C. London

D. Lilongwe

> Process of Elimination can help earn you valuable points on the MCAS.

You probably got this question right, even if you had no idea that there was a country named Malawi. How did you do that? First, you used the answer choices to help you out. Rather than asking yourself, "What do I know about Malawi?" (since you probably have never even heard of it), you looked at the answer choices. Second, you eliminated choices you knew were wrong. For instance, you probably know where Washington, Paris, and London are — and you know they aren't in Malawi. Therefore you crossed off choices **A**, **B**, and **C**. This left choice **D**. So even without knowing a thing about Malawi, you still got the right answer.

How does this work with math? Try this problem:

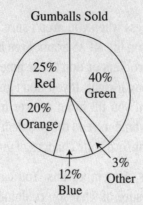

Gumballs Sold

The chart above shows the percentage of each color gumball sold during a certain month. If there were 400 gumballs sold that month, how many would you expect to be green?

A. 40

B. 110

C. 160

D. 200

You could calculate 40 percent of 400. But you could also solve this by POE. By looking at the chart, we can see that green gumballs are much more than $\frac{1}{4}$ of all gumballs sold. But choice A is far less than $\frac{1}{4}$ of 400, and choice B is just barely bigger than $\frac{1}{4}$ of 400. Choice D, however, is much too big because it's half of 400. Therefore, the answer must be C.

Of course, you won't always be able to eliminate all three wrong choices. But remember that every time you eliminate one wrong answer choice, you significantly improve your chances of picking the correct answer. Using POE aggressively will help you guess well, and it will earn you a lot of points on the multiple-choice portion of the test.

Ballparking

Even if you don't know how to get the correct answer, you can often eliminate a couple of choices that are unreasonable (too big or too small) or choices that aren't "in the ballpark." This is what we just did on that gumball example on the previous page; we call it Ballparking; it's a version of POE. To Ballpark on a question, look at the answer choices you are given to see whether any of them are much too large or much too small to be correct. Eliminate any choice that is out of the ballpark.

> You can eliminate any answer choice that's out of the Ballpark!

Have a look at this example:

Irene is going to buy a new car that she wants to have painted. The dealer tells her that the price of the paint job is one-fifth the price of the car. If the total cost of the car and the paint job is $4,800, what is the price of the car?

A. $2,000

B. $3,000

C. $4,000

D. $4,250

Let's begin by Ballparking. The question says that the cost of the paint job is one-fifth of the price of the car. Since $2,000 is less than half of the final price of $4,800, and the cost of the paint job is less than the price of the car, we know that choice **A** is far too small. Eliminate it. If we get no further with this problem, we can take an educated guess from among the remaining choices.

Using the answer choices

But we're not quite finished with this problem. What's the easiest way to figure out which of the remaining choices is the right answer? Instead of trying to solve the question alone, we can use the remaining answer choices to make the work much easier. After all, there are only three answers left, and one of them must be right. We can simply try each of those answers until we find the one that works. The only rule to using the answer choices is: *Stay organized!* The best way to organize your information is to put it neatly in a chart next to the answer choices as you work out each one of them. So let's start by making a chart:

	Price of Car	Price of Paint Job	Total Cost
Choice A	(eliminated)		
Choice B	$3,000		
Choice C	$4,000		
Choice D	$4,250		

Now as we try each answer choice, we can fill out our chart and see which of them gives us the correct total cost of $4,800.

Could choice **B**, $3,000, be the answer? Let's test it out. If we assume that the price of the car is $3,000, then the price of the paint job is $\frac{1}{5}$ of $3,000, or $600. The total cost would then be $3,600. But the problem says that the total cost should be $4,800. Therefore choice **B** cannot be the answer.

Could choice C, $4,000, be the answer? If we assume that the price of the car is $4,000, then the price of the paint job is $\frac{1}{5}$ of $4,000, or $800. The total cost would then be $4,800. This is exactly what the problem says it should be, so choice **C** is the answer.

	Price of Car	Price of Paint Job	Total Cost
Choice A	(eliminated)		
Choice B	$3,000	$600	$3,600
Choice C	$4,000	$800	$4,800
Choice D	$4,250	$850	$5,100

Write it Down!

When in doubt, write it out!

One of the biggest mistakes testers make is trying to do the work in their heads. You may think it's faster, but in the long run, it's not. If you try to do work in your head, you might miss a step, then try to figure out where you went wrong, then try it again, and wind up going around in circles.

Testers don't lose time by writing down their work; rather, they lose time by going in mental circles because they can't keep track of everything in their heads, especially when you factor in the pressure of such an important test. So get in the habit of writing everything down. This will serve you well especially on the open-response questions, where many students don't get full credit simply because they forget to show their work.

Read Carefully

The single biggest source of mistakes on standardized tests comes from students not comprehending the question. If you don't really understand what the question is asking, you may do all sorts of interesting calculations only to end up answering something that you weren't asked. Make sure you are *absolutely clear* on what the question is asking before you start trying to answer it.

Take bite-sized pieces

Many of the multiple-choice questions you'll see are long word problems. It's easy to get confused if you try to solve the question all at once. The best way to approach these questions is by taking "bite-sized pieces." Read each sentence, one at a time. Underline important information. As soon as you can solve one piece of the problem, go ahead and solve it. Then add on the next piece, until you have the final answer. Let's see this in action:

Janice delivers 5 papers every day from Monday through Friday, and 8 papers every Saturday and Sunday. If she works for 6 weeks, how many papers will she deliver?

A. 150

B. 240

C. 246

D. 254

Let's take this one step at a time. If Janice delivers 5 papers every day from Monday through Friday, that makes 25 papers. If she delivers 8 on Saturday and Sunday, that's another 16, for a total of 41 per week.

> Do long multiple-choice problems one step at a time, taking bite-sized pieces.

Now let's look at the next sentence. If she works for 6 weeks, then she will deliver 6 times 41 papers, which makes a grand total of 246. Therefore the answer is **C**. The way to make sure you don't get lost in a complicated problem like this one is to do your work in bite-sized pieces.

Answering Open-response Questions

Remember this example of an open-response question from earlier?

The price of a rare coin was $120 in 1990. Each year from 1990 to 1998, the price of the coin is increased by 5 percent over the price from the previous year.

a. What was the price of the coin in 1991? Show how you found your answer.

b. What was the price of the coin in 1994? Show how you found your answer.

c. What is the earliest year in which the price of the coin was at least $\frac{1}{3}$ greater than in 1990? Show how you found your answer.

Since a good deal of your points come from the open-response questions, it's important to know on what you'll be graded. For each open-response question, the graders are given a "scoring rubric," which tells them what would count as a 4-point response, a 3-point response, a 2-point response, a 1-point response, and a 0-point response. A scoring rubric for the above problem would look something like this:

Score	Description
4	Student demonstrates comprehensive understanding of repeated percentages by implementing correct procedures with consistent accuracy.
3	Student demonstrates sound understanding of repeated percentages by implementing correct procedures with only minor errors.
2	Student demonstrates some understanding of repeated percentages by implementing correct procedures at least once.
1	Student completes at least one correct computation using percentages
0	Response is blank, incorrect, or irrelevant.

In plain old English, here's what this means:

- You score a 4 if you show all of the right steps and get all the right answers.

- You score a 3 if you show all of the right steps, but you make a mistake somewhere and don't get exactly the right answers.

- You score a 2 if you show the right steps some of the time, but not always.

- You score a 1 if somewhere on the page you have a correct calculation, whether you show your steps or not.

- You score a 0 if your response is blank, totally incorrect, or irrelevant.

On open-response questions, SHOW YOUR WORK! LABEL ALL PARTS! You might pick up points even if your actual answer is incorrect!

So, what would a 4-point response look like?

a. $\begin{array}{l} 1990 \\ \$120 \end{array}$ $\dfrac{5}{100}$ X $\$120 = \$6$ so worth $\boxed{\$126 \text{ in } 1991}$

b. $\begin{array}{l} 1991 \\ \$126 \end{array}$ $\dfrac{5}{100}$ X $\$126 = \$6.30$ so worth $\$132.30$ in 1992

$\begin{array}{l} 1992 \\ \$132.30 \end{array}$ $\dfrac{5}{100}$ X $\$132.30 = \$6.62$ so worth $\$138.92$ in 1993

$\begin{array}{l} 1993 \\ \$138.92 \end{array}$ $\dfrac{5}{100}$ X $\$138.92 = \$6.95$ so worth $\$145.87$ in 1994

$\boxed{\begin{array}{l} 1994 \\ \$145.87 \end{array}}$

c. $\dfrac{1}{3}$ more than $\$120$

$\dfrac{1}{3}$ of $\$120 = \$40$ so need a value larger than or equal to $\$160$

From part (b)
we know the coin was worth $\$145.87$ in 1994

$\begin{array}{l} 1994 \\ \$145.87 \end{array}$ $\dfrac{5}{100}$ X $\$145.87 = \$7.29$ so worth $\$153.16$ in 1995

$\begin{array}{l} 1995 \\ \$153.16 \end{array}$ $\dfrac{5}{100}$ X $\$153.16 = \$7.66$ which makes the price bigger than $\$160$

$\boxed{\text{in } 1996}$

You could still get 3 points if you made a simple mathematical error anywhere in your work; if a few parts were correct—say, parts *a.* and *b.*—you could have scored a 2. If only part 1 was correct, you would have gotten a score of 1. If you didn't write anything, or if the grader can't find anything that resembles a correct mathematical operation, you will receive a score of 0.

Part II

Subject Review

Chapter 3

Number Sense

One of the general ideas that the MCAS math exam is designed to test is your understanding of number sense. What does "number sense" mean? It means understanding the basic properties of numbers: Which numbers are larger than others, what happens to certain numbers when you multiply them by other numbers, or square them, and so on.

First, let's review the basics.

Definitions

Integers are numbers that have no fractional or decimal parts. Examples of integers are −10, −3, −1, 2, 10, 23, and 50. 0 is also an integer.

Rational numbers are numbers that can be expressed as a ratio of two integers: $-\frac{3}{1}$, $-\frac{1}{5}$, 0, $\frac{1}{2}$, $\frac{1}{3}$, 5, and so on. When rational numbers are put into decimal form, they will either have a finite number of digits after the decimal point (.5) or be repeating decimals $(.3\overline{333})$. A number that cannot be expressed as the ratio of two integers and whose decimal form does not come to an end or have a repeating decimal is *irrational*. Irrational numbers include π and $\sqrt{2}$.

Positive numbers are numbers larger than 0. Zero itself is *not* positive. Examples of positive numbers are $\frac{1}{2}$, 1, 2.33, and 5.

Negative numbers are numbers less than 0. Zero itself is *not* negative. Examples of negative numbers are $-\frac{1}{2}$, –1, –2.33, and –5.

Zero is considered neutral; it is neither positive nor negative.

Even numbers are integers that can be divided by 2 with no remainder. Examples of even numbers are –4, –2, 0, 2, 4, and 6. Note that 0 *is* even (even though it is neither positive nor negative!).

Odd numbers are integers that cannot be divided by 2 evenly. Examples of odd numbers are –3, –1, 1, 3, 5, and 7.

Factors are the numbers by which a number can be divided. For example, factors of 12 are the numbers by which 12 can be divided. The easiest way to find them is in pairs. Factors of 12 can be written as 1×12, 2×6, or 3×4. Therefore 12 can be divided by 1, 2, 3, 4, 6, and 12. These are the factors of 12.

Multiples are all the numbers that can be divided by a given number. For example, the multiples of 12 are the numbers that can be divided by 12. The easiest way to find these numbers is to count up by 12: $12 \times 1 = 12$; $12 \times 2 = 24$; $12 \times 3 = 36$ . . . . So the first three positive multiples of 12 are 12, 24, and 36. However, we can keep counting up by 12s forever: 12, 24, 36, 48, 60, 72, 84 . . . . *All* of these numbers are multiples of 12.

Hint: If you tend to confuse factors and multiples, remember this tip: **Factors are few; Multiples are many**. There are only a few factors for any given number. But there are always an infinite number of multiples!

Prime numbers are numbers that can be divided only by 1 and themselves. The first six prime numbers are 2, 3, 5, 7, 11, and 13. Note that 0 and 1 are *not* prime numbers, and that 2 is the only even prime number.

The *reciprocal* of a number is simply 1 divided by that number. The reciprocal of 3 is $\frac{1}{3}$, and the reciprocal of $\frac{1}{3}$ is 3. The product (multiplication) of a number and its reciprocal is always 1. You might have heard this called "flipping" a number.

The *absolute value* of a number is the distance from 0 to that number. In other words, it is simply that number's positive value. The absolute value of 6 is 6, and the absolute value of –6 is 6. Absolute value is indicated with two bars around a number, like this: $|-6|$.

A *variable* is any unknown quantity, which is usually indicated by a letter such as x or y. In the expression $3x + 4y$, the letters x and y are the variables and the numbers 3 and 4 are called their *coefficients*.

Decimals and Fractions

Decimals and fractions are two different ways of writing the same number. It's important to know how to convert from one to the other without your calculator because you may be asked a question that requires you to change the form of a number from fraction to decimal or vice-versa.

Converting decimals to fractions

Remember the names of the decimal places?

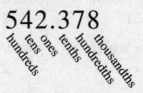

If you remember the names of the decimal places, then converting from decimal to fraction is easy. The digit 3 in the tenths place is the same thing as three-tenths, or $\frac{3}{10}$. The digit 7 in the hundredths place is the same as seven-hundredths, or $\frac{7}{100}$. The digit 8 in the thousandths place is the same as eight-thousandths, or $\frac{8}{1000}$. This gives us an easy way to convert from decimal to fraction form: Simply read the decimal out loud, and this will tell you how it should look as a fraction:

.6 is "six-tenths," which is equal to $\frac{6}{10}$

.54 is "fifty-four-hundredths," which is equal to $\frac{54}{100}$

Converting fractions to decimals

To convert a fraction to a decimal, all you have to do is divide the top number by the bottom number. You can do this either with your calculator or by using long division. For instance, $\frac{4}{5}$ is just 4 divided by 5, or .8. However, often there's an even easier way: If you can make the bottom number into a power of 10, you can use the same operation as we used above to convert a decimal to a fraction, but in reverse. For example, by multiplying both the top and bottom by 2, we can convert the fraction $\frac{4}{5}$ into $\frac{8}{10}$. And we know that $\frac{8}{10}$ is eight-tenths, which is .8. Neat, huh? This gives us an easy way to convert many fractions such as:

$$\frac{2}{25} = \frac{8}{100} = \text{eight-hundredths} = .08$$

$$\frac{3}{20} = \frac{15}{100} = \text{fifteen-hundredths} = .15$$

Remember, if you are using a calculator, put the top number into the calculator *first*.

Positive, Negative, Even, and Odd

In case you've forgotten, here are the rules for the product and quotient of positive and negative integers:

positive ÷ positive = positive   positive × positive = positive
2 ÷ 2   = 1   2 × 2   = 4

positive ÷ negative = negative   positive × negative = negative
2 ÷ –2   = –1   2 × –2   = –4

negative ÷ negative = positive   negative × negative = positive
–2 ÷ –2   = 1   –2 × –2   = 4

Another set of properties that you may need to know are the sums and products of even and odd integers:

even + even = even
2 + 2   = 4

even + odd = odd
2 + 3   = 5

odd + odd = even
3 + 3   = 6

even × even = even
2 × 2   = 4

even × odd = even
2 × 3   = 6

odd × odd = odd
3 × 3   = 9

Don't worry about memorizing these rules; instead, you should be able to recreate them for yourself just as we did above. Just pick some simple numbers like –3, –2, 2, and 3, and try them!

Remember: On exponent problems, when in doubt, expand it out!

Exponents

Exponents are just a shorthand way of writing multiplication. 2^3 is just a way of writing $2 \times 2 \times 2$. If you are ever troubled by an exponent problem, you can often write out the problem. When in doubt, expand it out!

You will probably not see many questions that involve exponents on the MCAS, but it's good to know the basic rules of exponents:

- When you multiply numbers with the same base, add the exponents:

$$3^4 \times 3^3 = 3 \times 3 \times 3 \times 3 \times 3 \times 3 \times 3 = 3^7$$

- When you divide them, subtract the exponents:

$$\frac{3^4}{3^3} = \frac{3 \times 3 \times 3 \times 3}{3 \times 3 \times 3} = 3^1$$

- If you raise an exponent to a power, multiply the exponents:

$$(3^2)^3 = 3 \times 3 \times 3 \times 3 \times 3 \times 3 = 3^6$$

- When several numbers are in parentheses, the exponent outside the parentheses must be distributed to all of the numbers inside:

$$(3y)^2 = 3^2 y^2 = 9y^2$$

There are, however, some special rules to exponents that you may be required to know for the MCAS. These special rules involve raising numbers to the powers of 0 and 1, and negative or fractional numbers raised to powers.

- Any number to the zero power is equal to 1: $3^0 = 1$

- Any number to the first power equals itself: $3^1 = 3$

- Any negative number raised to an *even* power becomes positive: $(-3)^2 = 9$. Be careful here: $(-3)^2 \neq -(3)^2$

- Any negative number raised to an *odd* power stays negative: $(-3)^3 = -27$

> Negative numbers raised to an even power are positive, and negative numbers raised to an odd power are negative.

Because we know that any negative number raised to an even power (such as 2) will become positive, and any negative number raised to an odd power (such as 3) will stay negative, we can know whether the number is even or odd, even if we can't calculate the value of that number. For instance, we know that -10675^4 will be positive, and -10675^5 will be negative.

This is all you will need to know to solve many "number sense" problems.

Finally, note that fractions between 0 and 1 have a funny property when you raise them to a power. Most numbers get bigger when you raise them to a power, and the bigger the power, the bigger the number. For example:

$$2^2 = 4, \ 2^3 = 8, \ 2^4 = 16, \text{ etc.}$$

> Fractions between 0 and 1 get *smaller* when you raise them to a power.

But when you raise a fraction between 0 and 1 to a power, the number gets smaller. And the bigger the power, the smaller the number becomes:

$$\left(\frac{1}{2}\right)^2 = \frac{1}{4}, \ \left(\frac{1}{2}\right)^3 = \frac{1}{8}, \ \left(\frac{1}{2}\right)^4 = \frac{1}{16}, \text{ etc.}$$

Square Roots

Square root is just the opposite of raising a number to the second power:

$$\sqrt{25} = 5, \text{ since } 5^2 = 25$$

As with exponents, you will probably not see many problems on the MCAS exam that deal with square roots. However, there is a special rule that you should know. Just as with exponents, fractions between 0 and 1 have a funny property when you take their square roots.

Fractions between 0 and 1 get *bigger* when you take their square root.

Most numbers get *smaller* when you take their square root:

$$\sqrt{16} = 4$$

But when you take the square root of a number between 0 and 1, the number gets *bigger*:

$$\sqrt{\frac{1}{9}} = \frac{1}{\sqrt{9}} = \frac{1}{3}$$

Plugging In

You've probably noticed that in a number of cases, we've been simply trying sample numbers to see what happens when we add, multiply, or find a square root. We call this technique Plugging In, and it's an important test-taking technique that will come in handy for a few problems on the MCAS exam. Whenever you have a problem with a variable (an unknown quantity) in the answer choices, you can make the problem much easier to solve by Plugging In a number for that variable everywhere in the problem.

Take control by Plugging In your own numbers anytime numbers are missing from the problem.

Let's see how this technique works by looking at the following problem:

If $0 < x < 1$, then which of the following has the greatest value?

A. x

B. x^2

C. x^3

D. $\frac{1}{x}$

Rather than doing a problem like this in your head or trying to solve it algebraically, the easiest and fastest way to solve it is to plug in a number for x. When we pick a number for x, we have to make sure that it is between 0 and 1, according to the restriction in the problem. So let's try $x = \frac{1}{2}$. If we make every x in the problem into $\frac{1}{2}$, the problem now reads:

. . . which of the following has the greatest value?

A. $\left(\dfrac{1}{2}\right)$

B. $\left(\dfrac{1}{2}\right)^2$

C. $\left(\dfrac{1}{2}\right)^3$

D. $\dfrac{1}{\frac{1}{2}}$

Now we can easily solve the problem. Which has the greatest value? Choice **A** equals $\dfrac{1}{2}$, choice **B** equals $\dfrac{1}{4}$, choice **C** equals $\dfrac{1}{8}$, and choice **D** equals 2. So choice **D** is the greatest.

If you are given values in the answer choices, rather than picking your own number to plug in, simply try Plugging In the answer choices until you find the one that works. Take a look at this problem:

If $x^2 < x$, which of the following could be the value of x?

A. 4

B. 1

C. 0

D. $\dfrac{1}{4}$

In this case, we should try Plugging In each of the answer choices for x until we find the one that works. Let's start with **A**. If x is equal to 4, is $x^2 < x$? 16 is greater than 4, so we can eliminate choice **A**. How about **B**? If x is equal to 1, is $x^2 < x$? 1 is equal to 1, so we can eliminate choice **B** as well. Now let's try **C**. If x is equal to 0, is $x^2 < x$? 0 is not less than 0, so we can eliminate choice **C**. Even though we already know what the answer has to be, let's check choice **D** just to be sure. If x is equal to $\dfrac{1}{4}$, is $x^2 < x$? $\dfrac{1}{16}$ is, in fact, less than $\dfrac{1}{4}$, so this is our answer.

Now try the following exercise:

Exercise 3.1 (answers on page 115)

a. What is .046 in fraction form?

b. What is $\dfrac{3}{5}$ in decimal form? (Don't use your calculator!)

c. What is $\dfrac{2}{50}$ in decimal form? (Don't use your calculator!)

d. What is $5075^0 \times 18^1$?

e. What is $\sqrt{36,501^0}$?

1   Which of the following is rational but not an integer?

   A. $\sqrt{10}$

   B. $\dfrac{4}{2}$

   C. $\dfrac{1}{3}$

   D. 5

2   The product of a negative odd integer and a positive even integer will be:

   A. positive and even

   B. positive and odd

   C. negative and even

   D. negative and odd

3   Which of the following is between $\dfrac{1}{50}$ and $\dfrac{4}{20}$?

   A. .015

   B. .067

   C. .24

   D. .40

4   Which of the following is greater than 0.338?

    A. .083

    B. .33

    C. .34

    D. .32889

5   The decimal .71 is between

    A. $\dfrac{3}{5}$ and $\dfrac{4}{5}$

    B. $\dfrac{1}{2}$ and $\dfrac{3}{5}$

    C. $\dfrac{3}{4}$ and $\dfrac{7}{8}$

    D. $\dfrac{1}{7}$ and $\dfrac{7}{10}$

6   Which of the following has the greatest value?

    A. $(-105)^{15}$

    B. $(-105)^{14}$

    C. $(55)^{12}$

    D. $(-55)^{12}$

7   If $0 < x < 1$, then which of the following has the greatest value?

    A. $5x$

    B. $5\dfrac{1}{x}$

    C. $\dfrac{x}{5}$

    D. x^5

8   If $0 < y < 1$, which of the following statements must be true?

   A. $y^2 < y < \sqrt{y}$

   B. $y < y^2 < \sqrt{y}$

   C. $\sqrt{y} < y < y^2$

   D. $y < \sqrt{y} < y^2$

9   If x is an odd negative integer, y is an even positive integer, and z is the product of x and y, which of the following is always true?

   A. z is a fraction

   B. z is an odd integer

   C. z is divisible by 3

   D. z is less than 0

Equations and Inequalities

An *equation* is a statement that contains an *equals* sign, such as $3x + 5 = 17$. To solve an equation, you want to get the variable x alone on one side of the equation, and everything else on the other side.

The first step is to put all of the variables on one side of the equation and all of the numbers on the other side, using addition and subtraction. As long as you perform the same operation on both sides of the equals sign, you aren't changing the value of the variable.

Then you can divide both sides of the equation by the *coefficient*, which is the number in front of the variable. If that number is a fraction, you can multiply everything by its reciprocal. For example:

$$3x + 5 = 17$$

Remember: The rule of equations is whatever you do to one side of the equation, you must also do to the other side.

$$
\begin{aligned}
3x + 5 &= 17 \\
-5 \quad &\quad -5 \qquad \text{Subtract 5 from each side.}\\
3x &= 12 \\
\div 3 \quad &\quad \div 3 \qquad \text{Divide 3 from each side.}\\
x &= 4
\end{aligned}
$$

An *inequality* is any statement with one of these signs:

< (less than)

> (greater than)

≤ (less than or equal to)

≥ (greater than or equal to)

You can solve inequalities in the same way you solve equations, with one exception:

> Whenever you multiply or divide an inequality by a negative value, you must change the direction of the inequality sign.

This means that when you multiply or divide by a negative value, < becomes >, and ≤ becomes ≥. For example:

$$3x + 5 > 17$$

$3x + 5$	$>$	17
-5		-5	Subtract 5 from each side.
$3x$	$>$	12
$\div 3$		$\div 3$	Divide each side by 3.
x	$>$	-4

In this case, we subtracted 5, but we didn't multiply or divide by a negative value, so the direction of the sign should not change. However, if we were to divide by a negative value, we would need to change the direction of the sign:

$$-3x + 5 > 17$$

$-3x + 5$	$>$	17
-5		-5	Subtract 5 from each side.
$-3x$	$>$	12
$\div -3$		$\div -3$	Divide each side by -3.
x	$<$	4

Percents

Percent just means "divided by 100." So 20% is the same thing as $\frac{20}{100}$. This, in turn, reduces to $\frac{1}{5}$, or .2. Likewise, 8% = $\frac{8}{100} = \frac{2}{25}$ or .08.

The easiest way to convert percent problems into simple math is to use the following "dictionary" to translate the sentence word for word:

When You See	Write
Percent	$\dfrac{}{100}$ (divide by 100)
Of	$\times$ (multiplication)
What	x, y, or any other variable
Is/Are/Makes	$=$

Here's how it works:

8% of 10	becomes	$\dfrac{8}{100} \times 10$, or .8
10% of 80	becomes	$\dfrac{10}{100} \times 80$, or 8
What is 5% of 50?	becomes	$x = \dfrac{5}{10} \times 50$, so $x = 25$

Special rule about percents

If you take 10% off of a number, and then add 10% to the resulting number, do you get the number with which you started? No. Why?

Let's find out with an actual number. Suppose we start with the number 200. To reduce it by 10%, we first find 10% of 200:

$$10\% \text{ of } 200 = \frac{10}{200} \times 200 = 20$$

This means that to decrease 200 by 10%, we subtract 20. When we subtract 20 from 200, we get 180. Now what happens if we increase the resulting number, 180, by 10%? To increase 180 by 10%, first find 10% of 180:

$$10\% \text{ of } 180 = \frac{10}{100} \times 180 = 18$$

This means that to increase 180 by 10%, we increase it by 18, so our final number is 198. Notice that by subtracting 10% and then adding 10%, we did not get back to our original value of 200.

Now take a look at the following problem:

The price of a pair of shoes is reduced by 20% during a sale. If the sale price of the shoes is $60, what was the original price of the shoes before the sale?

You might be tempted to answer $72 because increasing $60 by 20% gives you $72. But we know that can't be right: If you reduce a number by 20% to get $60, you won't get back to that number by adding 20% to $60. So how can we solve it? By translating our question into math according to the above directions.

We want to know what number, when we subtract 20% from it, makes 60. If we translate this question word for word, we get:

$$x - \frac{20}{100}x = 60$$

which becomes

$$x - .2x = 60$$

or

$$.8x = 60$$

Divide both sides by .8 to solve for x. Go ahead and use your calculator to solve for $\frac{60}{.8}$, which equals $75.

Percent increase/decrease

One kind of percent problem you may find on the MCAS is one that asks you to determine the percentage increase or decrease from one number to another. Take a look at this problem:

Sales in Bob's Department Store, 1990 and 1991

Item	1990	1991
Shirts	500	600
Pants	600	750
Ties	1,200	1,400
Belts	700	750

Which item showed the greatest percent increase in sales from 1990 to 1991?

A. Shirts

B. Pants

C. Ties

D. Belts

Whenever a problem asks for percentage increase or decrease, use the following formula:

$$\text{Percentage Increase or Decrease} = \frac{\textit{Amount of change}}{\textit{Original Amount}}$$

Let's use this formula to figure out the percentage increase for the items from Bob's Store. The amount of change in shirt sales is 100 since that is the increase in the number of shirts sold from 1990–1991. If we place this over the original number of shirts sold in 1990, which is 500, we see that the percentage increase is equal to $\frac{100}{500}$ or 20%. Let's do this for each of the items:

Shirts $\quad \frac{100}{500} = \frac{1}{5} = 20\%$

Pants $\quad \frac{150}{600} = \frac{1}{4} = 25\%$

Ties $\quad \frac{200}{1200} = \frac{1}{6} = 16.6\%$

Belts $\quad \frac{50}{700} = \frac{1}{14} = 7.1\%$

The greatest percentage increase is for pants, so the answer is **B**.

Sometimes you'll have to repeat this more than once to figure out how quickly a number will increase or decrease over time, or how long it will take a number to double in size. Don't worry about getting into complex mathematics—just keep applying the formula.

Try this problem:

The price of a book goes up 10% per year. After how many years will its price have increased by at least 45%?

A. 2 years

B. 3 years

C. 4 years

D. 5 years

You might be tempted to pick **D** in this case, but let's work it out. Suppose the book is originally priced at $100. If we increase this $100 by 10% each year, how fast does the price increase?

Plug In a number any time one is missing from a problem. It will make solving that problem much easier and faster.

Price	10%	New Price	% Change	Year
$100	$10	$110	10%	(Year 1)
$110	$11	$121	21%	(Year 2)
$121	$12.10	$133.10	33.1%	(Year 3)
$133.10	$13.31	$146.41	46.41%	(Year 4)

So, we don't have to wait 5 years for the price to increase over 45%. After only 4 years, the price has already risen 46%.

Estimation

Another skill tested on the MCAS exam is your ability to estimate information based on charts. Often, but not always, these problems will use words like "about" and "approximately" to tell you that they want you to estimate rather than figure out a numerical answer to a problem.

The trick to estimating is to use numbers you have a sense of (such as 2 times a number, 10 times a number, $\frac{1}{2}$ or $\frac{1}{4}$ of a number). Since you won't be able to calculate an exact answer to these problems, you will need to rely heavily on Process of Elimination and find the answer that comes *closest* to what you think the answer should be. Take a look at the following:

Company X Insurance

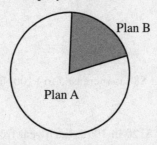

If 395 people buy insurance from Company X, approximately how many purchase plan B?

A. 40

B. 75

C. 100

D. 150

We don't have the information on the chart to actually calculate the number, so we need to estimate. To start, let's round 395 up to 400. Now, let's get a rough idea of how much of the shaded part of the circle represents Plan B. We know it's less than $\frac{1}{4}$. Since Plan B is less than $\frac{1}{4}$ of the circle, we know that it must be less than $\frac{1}{4}$ of 400, or less than 100. Now let's go to the answers and use POE: We can eliminate choices **C** and **D** because they are too big. It looks like choice **A** is going to be much too small—40 is only $\frac{1}{10}$ of 400, but the shaded area is more than $\frac{1}{10}$ of the circle. Therefore we can eliminate **A**, and we are left with choice **B**. That's all there is to it!

Now try out what you've just learned on the following problems.

Exercise 3.2 (answers on page 117)

a. Solve for x: $4x + 3 = 31$

b. Solve for x: $5x - 4 = 3x$

c. Solve for x: $5x - 4 > 4x$

d. In 1995, Marc's salary increased from $20,000 to $24,000. By what percent did his salary increase?

e. The price of a car increases by 30% per year. By what percent will its price have increased after 2 years?

f. What is 20% of 420?

g. 15 is 30% of what number?

h. If a dress originally priced at $80 is increased to $100, by what percent was the price of the dress increased?

The price of a rare coin was $120 in 1990. Each year from 1990–1998, the price of the coin was increased by 10% over the price from the previous year.

i. What was the price of the coin in 1991?

j. What was the price of the coin in 1994? Show how you found your answer.

k. What is the earliest year in which the price of the coin was at least $200? Show how you found your answer.

1   The population of Smalltown shrank from 1,200 inhabitants in 1960 to 800 inhabitants by
    1970. By approximately what percent did its population decrease from 1960–1970?

    A. 25%

    B. 30%

    C. 33%

    D. 35%

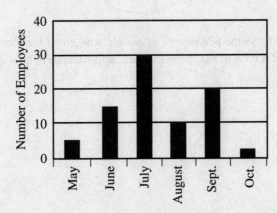

2   Each of the 80 employees at a company took a vacation during the months of May through
    October. The number of employees who took a vacation in each month is shown above in the
    chart. Approximately what percent of the employees took a vacation in the months of August
    through October?

    A. 30%

    B. 32%

    C. 35%

    D. 40%

Percentage of Votes
for Candidates W, X, Y, and Z

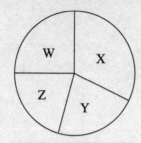

3   The chart above shows the percentage of people who voted for candidates W, X, Y, and Z in a
     recent election. If a total of 600 people voted, approximately how many voted for candidates Y
     or Z?

     A. 140

     B. 175

     C. 230

     D. 350

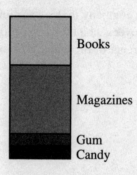

4   Sarah sells books, magazines, gum, and candy in her store. The chart above shows the percent-
     ages of each type of item she sold in January. If she sold 350 books in January, approximately
     how many magazines did she sell?

     A. 300

     B. 550

     C. 675

     D. 730

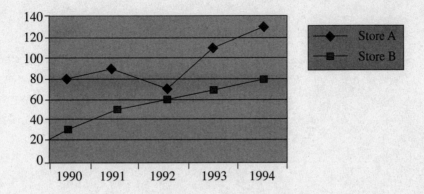

5   The chart above shows the number of shovels sold in two stores from 1990 to 1994. Which store had the greater percent increase in sales from 1990 to 1994? Explain how you got your answer.

Chapter 4

Geometry and Measurement

There's a lot of material to cover in this chapter, but the first part is review. Take your time now, and you'll find that you'll be better off on test day!

Lines, Angles, and Figures

You won't find many problems on the MCAS exam that test angles, triangles, squares, and circles, but you will probably see one or two, and it's important to master the basics so that you can solve the more complex problems you will see.

These formulas will be provided for you on your Formula Sheet, so don't worry about memorizing them. What *is* important, however, is knowing how to put these formulas into practice. We'll get to that part next.

You have to review the basics before you can do the more complex stuff.

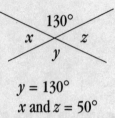

$$y = 130°$$
$$x \text{ and } z = 50°$$

The angles on any line must add up to 180 degrees. Angles across from each other when two lines cross (which are called *vertical angles*) are equal. In the figure above, we know that z must equal 50° since 130° + z must equal 180°. We know that y is 130 degrees since it is across from the angle 130°. We also know that x is 50° since it is across from z.

Area and perimeter

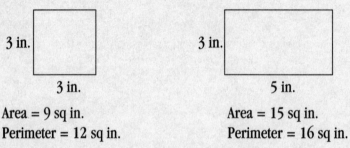

Area = 9 sq in.
Perimeter = 12 sq in.

Area = 15 sq in.
Perimeter = 16 sq in.

The *area* of a square, rectangle, or parallelogram is *base* × *height*. The *perimeter* of any figure is the sum of the lengths of its sides.

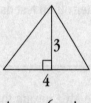

Area = 6 sq in.

The *area* of a triangle is $\frac{1}{2}$ *base* × *height*.

Angles

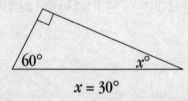

$$x = 30°$$

The sum of the angles inside a triangle must equal 180 degrees. If you know two of the angles in a triangle, you can always solve for the third. Since we know that two of the angles in the figure above are 90 degrees and 60 degrees, we can solve for the third angle.

There must be 180 degrees in a triangle.

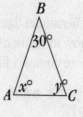

$$x = y = 75$$

Angles that are opposite equal sides must be equal. In this figure, we have an isosceles triangle. Since $\overline{AB} = \overline{BC}$, we know that angles x and y are equal. And since their sum must be 150 degrees (to make a total of 180 degrees when we add the last angle), they each must be 75 degrees.

Circles

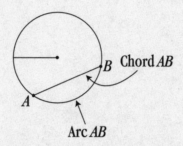

- The *radius* of a circle is the distance from the center to the edge of the circle.

- The *diameter* is the distance from one edge, through the center, to the other edge of the circle. The diameter will always be twice the measure of the radius.

- A *chord* is any line drawn from one edge of the circle to the other.

- An *arc* is any section of the circumference (the rim) of the circle.

- The *angles* inside a circle must add up to 360 degrees.

The *circumference* of a circle is the distance around the outside of the circle. The circumference is given by the formula $2\pi r$. The formula for the *area* of a circle is πr^2. (These are on your Formula Sheet if you forget them.)

Area = 64π
Circumference = 16π

Volume

Volume refers to the space inside of a three-dimensional figure, such as the space inside of a cube or a cylinder. All you need to know is how to figure out the volume of basic figures; you will be given the formulas you need for more complex figures.

The volume of a three-dimensional solid is *length × width × depth*.

Here's an example:

> John is filling a pool with dimensions 10 feet by 5 feet by 2 feet. If he adds a cubic foot of water every 5 seconds, how long will it take for him to fill the pool? Show your work.

First we need to find the volume of the pool. The volume of the pool is 10 × 5 × 2, or 100 cubic feet. This means that it takes 100 cubic feet of water to fill the pool. If John adds 1 cubic foot of water every 5 seconds, it will take 100 × 5, or 500 seconds, to fill the pool.

Problem-Solving with Figures

Whenever you have a diagram, ask yourself: *What else do I know?* Then, *write everything you can think of in your booklet*. You may not see right away why it's important, but write it down anyway. Chances are good that you will be making progress toward the answer, even without knowing it. Remember to label everything you know.

Here's an example:

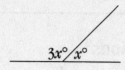

In the figure above, what is the value of x?

A. 30°

B. 40°

C. 45°

D. 60°

It may not be obvious how to go about solving this problem. But what do we know about this diagram? We have a line, and we know that the angles on a line always add up to 180°. Write that on your diagram.

Remember: Angles on a straight line must add up to 180 degrees.

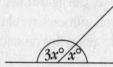

Now we can see that whatever x is, the sum of the angles marked $3x$ and x must equal 180°. So we can write an equation $3x + x = 180°$. This means that $4x = 180°$, so $x = 45°$. Thus, the answer is **C**.

Try this again with the following problem:

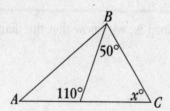

In triangle ABC above, $x =$

A. 30°

B. 40°

C. 50°

D. 60°

Notice that we don't know what angle A or angle B is. What *do* we know? Since the triangle on the left-hand side has one angle that measures 110 degrees, the angle next to it on the same straight line must be 70 degrees. That 70-degree angle, plus the 50-degree angle, add up to 120. Therefore $x = 60$ degrees. Choice **D** is the answer.

Remember: Angles in a triangle add up to 180 degrees.

Special Circle Rules

Circumference and revolutions

The circumference of a circle is important to know because it is also the distance the circle will roll in one revolution. Try the following problem:

A car has tires with a radius of 1 foot. If David drives the car forward such that the tires make 4 complete revolutions, how far will the car travel?

A. π feet

B. 4π feet

C. 8π feet

D. 12π feet

> A circle's circumference is what you use to figure out problems involving number of revolutions.

If the tire has a radius of 1 foot, we can figure out that its circumference will be 2π feet. This is how far it will roll with each revolution of the tires. If they turn 4 times, then the car will travel 4 times this distance, or 8π feet.

Chords

The special rule for chords is:

> Every chord in a circle is shorter than the diameter of that circle.

So if we know how long a chord is, we know that the diameter must be longer. Try the following problem:

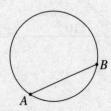

Mary measures chord *AB* of the circle above and finds that it is 6 inches long. What else must be true about this circle?

A. The radius of the circle is equal to 3.

B. The radius of the circle is less than 3.

C. The area of the circle is greater than 9π.

D. The circumference of the circle is greater than 9π.

Since we know that *AB* is a chord, we know that the diameter must be longer than it. So the diameter must be bigger than 6 inches long. This means that the radius must be bigger than 3.

This allows us to use POE to eliminate choices **A** and **B**. If the radius is bigger than 3, it might be 4 or 5. If the radius is 4, then the circumference becomes 8π, so we can eliminate **D**. This leaves only choice **C**.

A chord is always shorter than the diameter of a circle.

Arcs

The special rule for arcs is:

> The measure of an arc is always proportional to the inside angle that defines it.

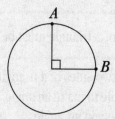

We can see that the angle in the figure above measures 90 degrees. This 90-degree angle is $\frac{1}{4}$ of all the angles in the circle because 90 degrees is $\frac{1}{4}$ of 360 degrees, and there are 360 degrees in a circle. Therefore, we know that the arc AB is equal to $\frac{1}{4}$ of the circumference of the circle.

Now try the following problem:

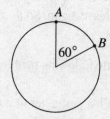

If the circle above has a radius of 4, what is the length of arc AB?

A. $\dfrac{4\pi}{3}$

B. 4π

C. 8π

D. $\dfrac{8\pi}{3}$

Since we know that the radius is 4, we can solve for the circumference of the circle, which will be 8π. Because the angle that forms arc AB measures 60 degrees, which is $\frac{1}{6}$ of the 360 degrees inside of a circle, we know that the arc AB must be equal to $\frac{1}{6}$ of the circumference of the circle. $\frac{1}{6}$ of 8π is the same as $\frac{8\pi}{6} = \frac{4\pi}{3}$.

Special Triangle Rules

One triangle rule that is often tested on the MCAS exam is the *third side* rule. The rule is:

> The sum of every two sides of a triangle must be greater than the third side.

Why? Look at it this way: If you had two sides of a triangle whose lengths were exactly as big as the third side, they wouldn't be able to make an angle. Therefore they must be bigger than the third side so that they can connect at an angle.

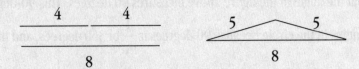

If the sum of two sides of the triangle were equal to the third side, as in the picture with sides 4, 4, and 8, we would not be able to form a triangle. At most we could combine the two short sides to make a straight line of length 8 and place it next to the third side. If we want to "raise" those other two sides to make an angle, they will have to be a bit longer, or else they will separate like a drawbridge and leave a gap. So to make a triangle, the other two sides will have to have a sum larger than 8.

With this rule in mind, let's look at the following problem:

Which of the following is a possible perimeter of a triangle with sides 5 and 8?

A. 15

B. 16

C. 17

D. 26

Let's use POE: Could the answer be **A**? If the perimeter is 15, this means that the sides must be 5, 8, and 2. But this is not a possible triangle since the sides 5 and 2 don't have a sum that is larger than 8. Choice **B** has the same problem. Choice **C** could work since a perimeter of 17 would mean that the sides would be 5, 8, and 4. These could be the sides of a triangle since the sum of any two of them are larger than the third. This makes **C** the answer. Just to be sure, let's see why **D** doesn't work. If the perimeter is 26, the sides would have to be 5, 8, and 13. However, the sides 5 and 8 aren't greater than the side of 13, so these can't be the sides of a triangle.

Similar triangles

Two triangles are *similar* if they have the same set of angles. And if two triangles are similar, then their sides will be proportional. This means that every side of one triangle will be in a fixed ratio with the corresponding side of the other triangle. Here is an example of similar triangles:

If two triangles have two equal angles, the triangles must be similar because the triangles' third angles have to be equal in order for the sum of the angles in each triangle to total 180 degrees.

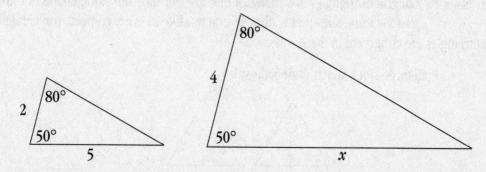

Since each triangle above has an angle that measures 50 degrees and an angle that measures 80 degrees, we know that these triangles are similar. Since the triangle on the right has a side 4 that corresponds with the side 2 on the triangle on the left, we know that every side of the triangle on the right must be twice the length of the corresponding side on the left triangle. So we can solve for x, which must be 10.

Note that if the two triangles are drawn such that they meet at vertical angles, then we need to know only that the triangles have one other angle of the same measure to conclude the triangles are similar. Try this problem:

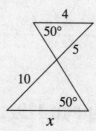

What is the value of x in the figure above?

A. 4

B. 6

C. 8

D. 10

These two triangles meet in the middle, so the angles where they meet are vertical angles and have the same measure. Even though we don't know the exact value of the angle, we know that it's the same for both triangles. Further, since each triangle has a 50-degree angle, we know that these triangles must each have the same set of angles. So they are similar triangles, and their sides are proportional. The sides opposite the 50-degree angle are 5 and 10, so we know that each side of the bottom triangle must be twice each side of the top triangle. Thus we know that x must be equal to 8, choice **C**.

Congruent triangles

> Congruent triangles are exactly the same size and shape.

Congruent triangles are triangles that are not only the same shape but are also the same size—that is, they're exactly alike in every respect. You can tell that triangles are congruent in three ways:

- If all three sides match (side-side-side)

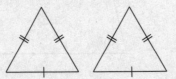

- If two angles and their included side match (angle-side-angle)

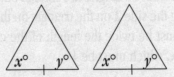

- If two sides and their included angle match (side-angle-side)

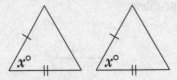

Now try the following exercise:

Exercise 4.1 (answers are on page 119)

a. The sides of a certain triangle are all integer values. If two sides of the triangle are 9 and 11, what is the smallest possible perimeter of the triangle?

b. What is the largest possible perimeter of a triangle with sides 9 and 11?

c. Three corners of a rectangle are at (2, 5), (−3, −4), and (2, −4). What is the area of the rectangle?

d. If the figure below is a rectangle, what is $x + y$?

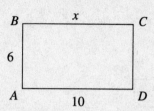

e. What is the area of the circle below? What is its circumference? If the circle makes 10 revolutions in a straight line, how far will it travel?

1. If $y = 35°$, what is the value of $x°$?

   A. 10°

   B. 15°

   C. 20°

   D. 25°

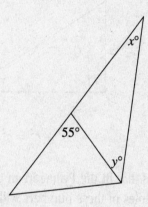

2. Which of the following are similar but not congruent?

A. □ □

B. ▱ ▭

C. △ △

D. ○ □

The Pythagorean theorem

Whenever you have a right triangle—a triangle with a 90-degree angle—you can use the Pythagorean theorem. The theorem says that the sum of the squares of the legs of the triangle (the sides next to the right angle) will equal the square of the hypotenuse (the side opposite the right angle).

Popular Pythagorean ratios include the 3:4:5 (and its multiples) and the 5:12:13 (and its multiples).

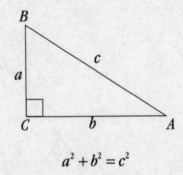

$$a^2 + b^2 = c^2$$

Two of the most common ratios that fit the Pythagorean theorem are 3:4:5 and 5:12:13. Since these are ratios, any multiples of these numbers will also work, such as 6:8:10, and 30:40:50.

Try the following examples:

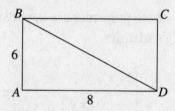

If *ABCD* is a rectangle, what is the perimeter of triangle *ABD*?

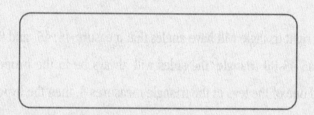

We can use the Pythagorean theorem to figure out the length of the diagonal of the rectangle: since it has sides 6 and 8, its diagonal must be 10. (If you remembered that this is one of those well-known Pythagorean ratios, you didn't actually have to do the calculations.) Therefore, the perimeter of the triangle is 6 + 8 + 10, or 24 units.

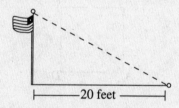

A cord is stretched from the top of a 15-foot flagpole to a point in the ground that is 20 feet away from the base of the flagpole. How long is the cord?

A. 20 feet

B. 23 feet

C. 25 feet

D. 30 feet

For this problem, we can do essentially the same thing. The length of the cord will be the hypotenuse of the triangle that has sides 20 and 15. Now use the Pythagorean theorem to solve for the hypotenuse. Or, maybe you noticed that 15 and 20 are the first two elements in a ratio of 3:4:5, so the hypotenuse will have to be 25, choice **C**.

Special Right Triangles

There are two right triangles whose properties are important to memorize. They are the 45-45-90 and the 30-60-90 right triangles.

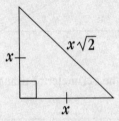

Remember: The ratio of the sides of a 45:45:90 triangle is $x:x:x\sqrt{2}$.

An isosceles right triangle will have angles that measure 45, 45, and 90 degrees. Whenever you have a 45-45-90 triangle, the sides will always be in the proportion $x:x:x\sqrt{2}$. This means that if one of the legs of the triangle measures 3, then the hypotenuse will be $3\sqrt{2}$.

This isosceles right triangle is important because it is half of a square. Memorizing the 45-45-90 triangle will allow you to easily find the diagonal of a square from its side, or find the side of a square from its diagonal.

Here's an example:

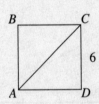

In the square above, what is the perimeter of triangle *ABC*?

In this square, we know that each of the triangles formed by the diagonal *AC* will be a 45-45-90 right triangle. Since the square has a side of 6, the diagonal will be $6\sqrt{2}$. Therefore, the perimeter of the triangle will be $6 + 6 + 6\sqrt{2}$, or $12 + 6\sqrt{2}$.

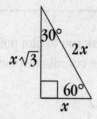

The other important right triangle to memorize is the 30-60-90 right triangle. This triangle has sides that are always in the ratio $x : x\sqrt{3} : 2x$. If the smallest side (the x side) of the triangle is 5, then the sides will measure 5, $5\sqrt{3}$, and 10. This triangle is important because it is half of an equilateral triangle, and allows us to find the height of an equilateral triangle.

Try the following:

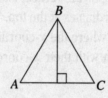

Triangle *ABC* above is equilateral, with sides of 4. What is its area?

A. 3 sq units

B. $4\sqrt{2}$ sq units

C. $4\sqrt{3}$ sq units

D. 8 sq units

We can divide *ABC* into two 30-60-90 triangles, each with a base of 2 and hypotenuse of 4. The height of *ABC* will be equal to the remaining side of these triangles. Since we know that the ratio of the sides of a 30-60-90 triangle is always $x : x\sqrt{3} : 2x$, we can determine that the sides of these smaller triangles must be $2 : 2\sqrt{3} : 4$. So the height of *ABC* is $2\sqrt{3}$. Now we can solve for the area, which is $\frac{1}{2} \times 4 \times 2\sqrt{3}$, or $4\sqrt{3}$ sq units. That's choice **C**.

The Coordinate Plane

Several of the questions on the MCAS will ask you to plot points, find the size of objects, or figure out what a line would look like on the coordinate plane. The coordinate plane looks like this:

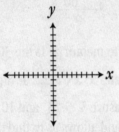

The x-axis is the horizontal axis and runs from negative x-coordinates on the left to positive x-coordinates on the right. The y-axis is the vertical axis and runs from negative y-coordinates at the bottom to positive y-coordinates at the top. The place where the two axes meet is called the *origin* and is the point where the x-coordinate and y-coordinate are each 0. Points on the plane are always given with their x-coordinate first, and their y-coordinate second.

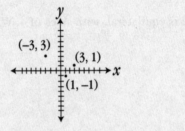

To plot point $(3, 1)$ we count three points to the right of the origin on the x-axis and one point up on the y-axis. Point $(-3, 3)$ will be three points to the left on the x-axis and three points up on the y-axis. Point $(1, -3)$ will be one point to the right on the x-axis and three points down on the y-axis.

Slope

Slope refers to the steepness of a line.

Remember: slope = $\dfrac{\text{rise}}{\text{run}}$

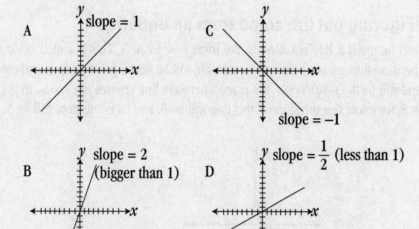

A line that goes up and to the right will have a positive slope. A slope that goes down and to the right will have a negative slope.

To estimate slopes, here's a handy tip: A line that goes up and to the right at a 45 degree angle, as in picture **A**, has a slope of 1. If the line goes up more steeply than this, as in picture **B**, it will have a slope greater than 1. If the line goes up less steeply, as in picture **D**, it will have a slope less than 1.

The slope formula is one that you *do* want to know by heart:

$$Slope = \frac{y_2 - y_1}{x_2 - x_1} = \frac{\textit{rise}}{\textit{run}} \text{ where } (x_1, y_1) \text{ and } (x_2, y_2) \text{ are points on the line.}$$

Figuring out the slope from points on a line

The easiest way to figure out your *rise* and your *run* for a line is to draw the right triangle that would get you from one point to the other, and then count the spaces.

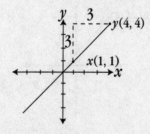

All we need to do is take any two points on the line above–in this case, points x (1, 1) and y (4, 4). Then we can draw a right triangle between them and measure the length of its legs. These will be the rise and run of the line. In this case, the rise is 3 and the run is 3, so the slope is $\frac{3}{3}$, or 1.

Figuring out the slope from an equation

Very often you will be given a line equation in the form $y = 5x + 3$. This is called *slope-intercept* form because the number before the x variable will be the slope of the line, and the number at the end will be the *y-intercept*, the place where the line crosses the y-axis. In the case of $y = 5x + 3$, we know that the slope of this line will be 5, and its y-intercept will be 3.

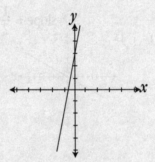

Now let's try graphing $y = -5x + 3$:

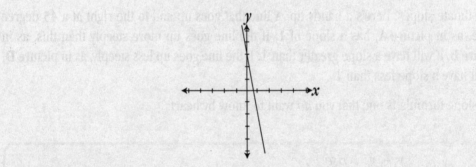

Notice that with any equation like this, you can figure out what the y-coordinate has to be for a certain x-coordinate, or vice-versa. Take the equation $y = -x + 1$. If you want to know what the y-coordinate will be when $x = 3$, just plug 3 into the equation in place of x, and we get $y = -2$. Likewise, if $x = -3$, then $y = 4$. We can then use these two points to draw the line $y = -x + 1$:

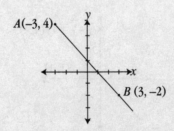

A(−3, 4)

B (3, −2)

If you aren't sure how a figure will look, the easiest way to proceed is to plug in some easy numbers (such as the numbers from −4 to 4) in place of x, and see what values you get for y. For instance, lets look at the equation $y = x^2$:

x	y
−4	16
−3	9
−2	4
−1	1
0	0
1	1
2	4
3	9
4	16

Now if we plot these points, we'll see what the shape looks like:

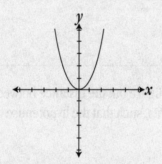

These types of graphed equations are called parabolas.

We'll see a lot more of these in our next chapter.

> **Remember:** Plug in whenever you see variables.

Slope of perpendicular lines

If you know the slope of any line, you can figure out the slope of the line that is perpendicular to it.

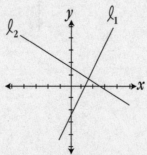

If a line l_2 is perpendicular to a line l_1, then the slope of l_2 will be the negative reciprocal of the slope of l_1. This means that if the slope of l_1 is 2, the slope of l_2 will be $-\dfrac{1}{2}$.

Distance between two points

Take a look at the following problem:

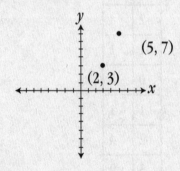

What is the distance between the points (2, 3) and (5, 7) shown above?

Drawing a right triangle is an easy way to figure out the distance between two points. Simply draw a right triangle between the two points, such that the hypotenuse of the right triangle is the distance between the points.

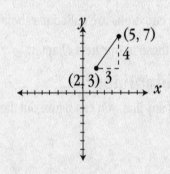

Then you can use the Pythagorean theorem to figure out the length of the hypotenuse, which is the distance between the two points. (If you've ever seen the *distance formula*, it's actually just another way of writing the Pythagorean theorem.) In this case, we can draw a right triangle that has sides 3 and 4. Therefore we know that the distance between these two points, which is the same as the hypotenuse of the right triangle, must be 5.

Transformations on the Coordinate Plane

Transformations are all the various ways you can change the position of points or figures on the coordinate plane. You may be asked to move them right or left (which is called *translation*) or flip them across an axis (called *reflection*) and draw the resulting figure on your grid. You will probably be asked to do at least one or two transformations on your MCAS exam. Be sure to do these carefully, and label each step along the way.

Translation

Translation refers to moving a figure up, down, left, or right on the coordinate plane.

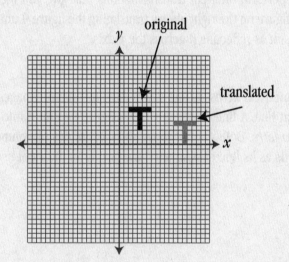

> Translation simply means moving a figure on the coordinate plane.

The chart above shows what happens if we take a shape and translate it 10 units to the right and 3 units down. To translate a figure, just count over, up, or down the number of points asked for in the problem.

Reflection

Reflection means exactly what it sounds like it means: It refers to how a figure would look in a mirror if the mirror were placed somewhere on the coordinate plane (usually on the *x*-axis or the *y*-axis).

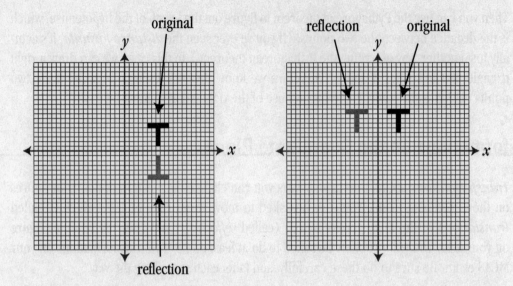

The picture on the left shows a figure translated across the *x*-axis; the picture on the right shows a figure reflected across the *y*-axis.

You can sometimes perform different transformations that give you the same final result. For instance, in the figure on the right above, translating the figure 9 units to the left would achieve the same result as reflecting it across the *y*-axis.

Symmetry

Two things are symmetrical across a line when they are mirror images of each other on opposite sides of that line. A line drawn through a figure to split it into identical halves is called a *line of symmetry*. Both graphs above show examples of symmetry. The graph on the left uses the *x*-axis as its line of symmetry; the graph on the right uses the *y*-axis as it's line of symmetry.

Symmetry appears on the MCAS exam in problems like this:

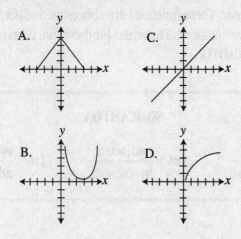

Which of the following has the y-axis as the line of symmetry?

A. Figure A

B. Figure B

C. Figure C

D. Figure D

A figure is symmetrical if it is identical on both sides.

Let's use POE. Which of these figures has a shape on one side of the y-axis that is identical with the shape on the other side? Certainly not **C** and **D**. While choice **B** has a kind of symmetry, it's not symmetrical across the y-axis, for which it would need to have both parts above the x-axis or below the x-axis. Therefore **A** is the best answer.

Trigonometry

Just as this book was going to press, slightly revised MCAS exam standards came out, which removed trigonometry from the test. Therefore, you probably won't have to know the following concept. However, these standards may be revised again next year, and this is something you'll want to learn soon anyway, so we'll discuss it. Even if they bring back trigonometry, you'll probably see at most one trigonometry problem on the MCAS exam, so it's not worth losing sleep over. These problems always involve finding the lengths of the sides of a right triangle given one of the angles.

For the angle marked Θ in the diagram below, there is one side which is *adjacent* to the angle, one side which is *opposite* the angle, and there is the *hypotenuse* of the triangle.

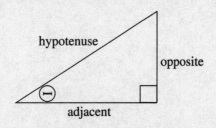

The three basic functions you will need to know are *sine*, *cosine*, and *tangent*. These functions are abbreviated $\sin\Theta$, $\cos\Theta$, and $\tan\Theta$. You can remember the formulas for these functions by memorizing the word SOHCAHTOA.

SOHCAHTOA

$$\sin = \frac{\text{opposite}}{\text{hypotenuse}} \qquad \cos = \frac{\text{adjacent}}{\text{hypotenuse}} \qquad \tan = \frac{\text{opposite}}{\text{adjacent}}$$

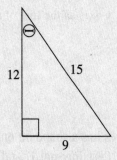

In the triangle above, what is the sine of angle Θ?

The sine of the angle will be the opposite side (9) over the hypotenuse (15), which makes $\frac{9}{15}$, or .6. If you wanted, you could use this information to find the measure of the angle by taking the inverse of the sine (marked on your calculator as $\sin^{-1}$), which comes to 36.87°.

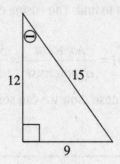

What is the cosine of angle Θ?

Likewise, the cosine of the angle will be the adjacent side (12) over the hypotenuse (15), which makes $\frac{12}{15}$, or .8. If you wanted, you could use this information to find the measure of the angle by taking the inverse of the cosine (marked on your calculator as cos⁻¹), which again comes to 36.87°.

We've just seen how you can use the lengths of the sides to figure out the angles of a right triangle. On the MCAS you'll probably be asked to do the opposite—to use the angles to figure out the lengths of the sides. If you know the measurement of one of the angles, you can use your calculator or your reference sheet to figure out its sine, cosine, or tangent, and this information can help you figure out the length.

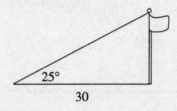

The figure above shows a straight cord that is stretched from the top of a flagpole to a spot on the ground 30 feet away from the base of the flagpole. If the angle at which the cord meets the ground is 25 degrees, how long is the cord?

A. 18.4 feet

B. 24.2 feet

C. 28.8 feet

D. 33.1 feet

We know that the cosine of 25 will be equal to the length of the adjacent side (30) over the hypotenuse, which is what we want to find. The cosine of 25 is roughly equal to .91. So we can write an equation:

$$.91 = \frac{Adjacent}{Hypotenuse} = \frac{30}{x}$$

where x is the length of the hypotenuse. Now we can solve: $x = 33.1$ feet.

Counterexamples

You will likely not see more than one of this type of problem. A *counterexample* is an example that shows that a certain statement or rule is *not* true. Whenever someone gives a rule that is supposed to apply to all cases, it only takes one counterexample to show that the rule does not hold. Here is an example of a counterexample question:

> A statement is made that for any four-sided figure, the lengths of its diagonals will be equal. Give an example of a figure that shows that this statement is not true.

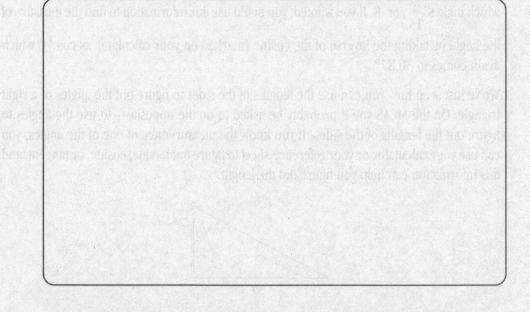

This question is asking you to produce an example that does not fit the above statement. In this case, we need to draw a four-sided figure whose diagonals are of different lengths. Play around with the figure until you find a counterexample. Any parallelogram that is not a rectangle will work:

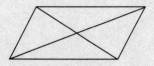

Another kind of counterexample problem involves *If . . . then* statements. Try the following problem:

> Jim's football coach tells Jim, "If you can run a mile in less than 6 minutes, then I will let you go home early." Which of the following would show the coach did not follow through with his statement?
>
> A. Jim runs a mile in less than 6 minutes, and his coach does not let him go home early.
>
> B. Jim runs a mile in less than 6 minutes, and his coach lets him go home early.
>
> C. Jim does not run a mile in less than 6 minutes, and his coach does not let him go home early.
>
> D. Jim does not run a mile in less than 6 minutes, and his coach lets him go home early.

Whenever you have a statement of the form "If *x*, then *y*," the way to find a counterexample is to find the case where *x is* true but *y is not* true.

The counterexample to the coach's statement to Jim that "If you can run a mile in less than 6 minutes, I will let you go home early" will be: "Jim runs a mile in less than 6 minutes, and the coach does *not* let him go home early." Which choice says this? Choice **A**.

Now let's try the following problems to help reinforce what we've just covered:

Exercise 4.2 (answers are on page 120)

a. What is the slope of a line that passes through points (2, 4) and (5, 10)?

b. What is the slope of a line that passes through points (–1, –1) and (4, 3)?

c. If a line is defined by the equation $x = 3y + 5$, what is the slope of the line?

> A counterexample simply contradicts the given information.

d. What is the slope of the line perpendicular to the line defined by $y = 2x + 3$?

e. What is the diagonal of a square with side 5?

f. If the diagonal of a square is $7\sqrt{2}$, what is the length of one side of this square? What is the area of this square?

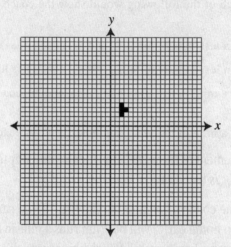

g. Look at the shape on the graph above. Transform it according to the following rules: First, the shape is reflected across the x-axis. Then it is reflected across the y-axis. Draw and label each step of this transformation on the grid below.

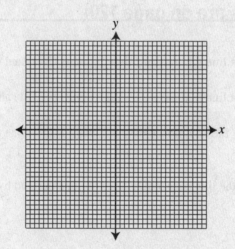

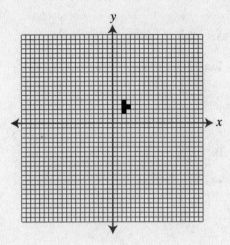

h. Look at the shape on the graph above. Transform it according to the following rules: Translate the shape up 5 units on the *y*-axis, and then reflect it across the *x*-axis. Draw and label each step of this transformation on the grid below.

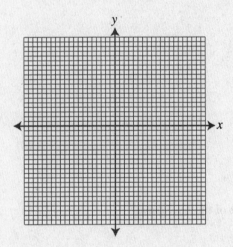

i. What is the distance between points (−1, 3) and (5, 11)?

j. A statement is made that for any prime number *n*, *n* + 2 will also be prime. Give an example of a number that shows this statement is *not* true.

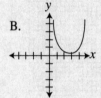

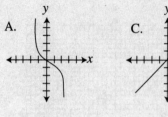

1   Which of the following shows a function that might be symmetrical across the line $x = 5$?

A.   Figure A

B.   Figure B

C.   Figure C

D.   Figure D

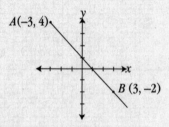

2   What is the slope of the line above?

A. -2

B. -1

C. $-\dfrac{1}{2}$

D. $\dfrac{1}{2}$

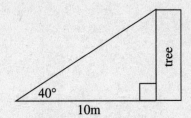

3 The figure above shows the flight path of an insect that flies from the ground to the top of a tree whose base is set at a distance of 10 meters. If the insect flies in a straight line at an angle of ascent of 40 degrees, how far does the insect fly?

A. 10.76 meters

B. 11.28 meters

C. 13.05 meters

D. 16.54 meters

Chapter 5

Patterns, Relations, and Functions

Some of the more complex problems on the MCAS exam involve functions and patterns. The idea that ties all these problems together is that in each case, one thing depends on another. While some of these problems may look strange, they test a few very basic principles. Once you learn those principles, you can solve any one of these problems.

Algebraic Relations

You may see a question or two on your MCAS exam that asks you to write an equation that expresses the relationship between two variables. If you see a problem of this type, don't try to write out the equation yourself. Simply read the equations in the answer choices, and use POE to eliminate the ones that don't quite fit.

Try this example:

> The number q is 7 less than 6 times the sum of k and 2. Which of the following expresses the relationship of q and k?
>
> A. $q = 6(k + 2) - 7$
>
> B. $q - 7 = 6k + 2$
>
> C. $q = 7 - 6(k + 2)$
>
> D. $6q = k + 2 - 7$

POE: Learn it. Live it. Love it.

We know that we need to take 7 away from something, so we can eliminate choice **C**. Further, we need to multiply the sum of *k* and 2 by 6. This will eliminate **B** and **D**. Since **A** is the only choice left, it must be the correct answer.

To help you write your equations, be sure to translate:

What it Says	What it Actually Means
sum	addition
difference	subtraction
product	multiplication
quotient	division
10 more than x	$x + 10$
10 less than x	$x - 10$
10 is more than x	$10 > x$
10 is less than x	$10 < x$

Expanding, Factoring, and Solving Quadratic Equations

Ah, factoring. You're likely to see at least one problem on the MCAS exam that asks you to do this sort of complex algebraic manipulation. Since it may have been a little while since you've done this, let's review.

Expanding

Most often you'll be asked to expand an expression simply by multiplying it out. When working with an expression of the form $(x + 3)(x + 4)$, multiply out using the following rule:

FOIL = First Outer Inner Last

Start with the first figure in each set of parenthesis: $x \times x = x^2$

Now do the two outermost figures: $x \times 4 = 4x$

Next, the two inner figures: $3 \times x = 3x$

Finally, the last figure in each set of parentheses: $3 \times 4 = 12$

Add them all together, and we get $x^2 + 4x + 3x + 12$, or $x^2 + 7x + 12$.

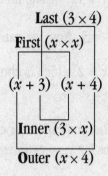

Last (3×4)

First $(x \times x)$

$(x + 3)$ $(x + 4)$

Inner $(3 \times x)$

Outer $(x \times 4)$

Factoring

If you ever see an expression of the form $x^2 + 7x + 12$ on the MCAS exam, there is a very good chance that you will be required to factor it. Here are the steps:

Step 1 Find the factors of the constant (in this case, 12).

Step 2 See which pair of factors you can either add or subtract to get the coefficient of x (in this case, 7).

Step 3 Put those factors into parentheses along with the appropriate signs.

How does this work for the expression $x^2 + 7x + 12$?

Step 1 We can factor 12 either as 1×12, 2×6, or 3×4.

Step 2 We can get 7 by taking $+3$ and adding $+4$, so put 3 and 4 into parentheses.

Step 3 Add the plus signs, since $+3$ and $+4$ together make 7.

$$x^2 + 7x + 12$$
$$(x \quad) (x \quad)$$
$$(x \quad 3) (x \quad 4)$$
$$(x + 3) (x + 4)$$

If you want to double-check your work, try expanding out $(x + 3)(x + 4)$, and you'll get the original expression.

Now try the following problem:

If $\dfrac{x^2 + 7x + 12}{(x + 4)} = 5$, then what is the value of x?

A. 1

B. 2

C. 3

D. 5

Since we know we can factor $x^2 + 7x + 12$, we should do so, and see what happens. When we factor it, we get $\dfrac{(x+3)(x+4)}{(x+4)} = 5$. Now we can cancel the $(x + 4)$, which leaves $x + 3 = 5$. Now we can solve for x: $x = 2$, which is choice **B**.

Solving quadratic equations

Sometimes you'll see an expression that you can factor contained within an equation. In this case, there will be two possible values for x, sometimes called the *roots* of the equation. To solve for x, use the following steps:

Step 1   Make sure that the equation is set equal to 0.

Step 2   Factor the equation.

Step 3   See which values for x will make either part of the equation equal to 0. For $(x + 3)$, if $x = -3$, then the value in parentheses will equal 0. For $(x - 3)$, if $x = 3$, then the value in parentheses will equal 0.

Try the following problem:

If $x^2 + 2x + 15 = 0$, then the possible values of x are:

A. 2 and 4

B. −13 and −4

C. 5 and −4

D. −5 and −3

Let's try the steps:

Step 1   The equation is already set equal to 0.

Step 2   We can now factor the left side of the equation, to get $(x + 5)(x - 3) = 0$.

Step 3   The two values for x that would fit this equation are −5 and −3. Therefore the answer is **D**.

Usually you'll be given a problem where the expression already equals 0; if not, you'll have to manipulate it so that it does:

If $x^2 + 7x + 15 = 3$, then the possible values of x are:

A. 3 and 4

B. −3 and −4

C. 3 and −4

D. −3 and 6

In this case, we'll need to subtract 3 from each side to make sure that the expression equals 0. When we subtract 3 from each side, we get

$$x^2 + 7x + 12 = 0$$

We can now factor the left side, to get

$$(x + 3)(x + 4) = 0$$

and the two values for x that would fit this equation are -3 and -4. Therefore, the answer is **B**.

Patterns

You may see one or two problems on the MCAS exam that involve patterns. Here's an example:

> On pattern questions, when in doubt, write it out!

> A store gives a door prize to its third customer, and to every fifth customer after that. Which of the following customers will get a door prize?
>
> A. the 62nd
>
> B. the 71st
>
> C. the 79th
>
> D. the 98th

Whenever you see a problem like this one, don't just stare at it hoping to see the pattern. Start working out the problem on paper, and after a few steps you should be able to see the pattern. If the third customer gets a prize, as does every fifth customer who follows, the list of customers who will get prizes should be numbers

$$3, 8, 13, 18, 23, 28, 33 \ldots \text{etc.}$$

So every number that ends in a 3 or an 8 will get a prize. Of the choices listed, only **D** ends with a 3 or an 8, so it must be the answer.

Functions

A function is a kind of relationship where one thing depends on another. For instance, if we know that every guest at a party brings two gifts, we can figure out how many gifts will be brought by any given number of guests. We can even write a formula:

Number of gifts = 2 × Number of guests

In function-language, this would be written as:

$$f(x) = 2x$$

To figure out the value of a function, all you have to do is plug in a value for x and solve. Try the following:

You can Plug In on function problems!

x	$f(x)$
3	12
4	19
5	28
6	39

Which of the following could be $f(x)$?

A. $f(x) = 4x$

B. $f(x) = x^2 + 3$

C. $f(x) = 5x - 3$

D. $f(x) = 5x + 3$

To solve this problem, plug the values of x in the chart into each of the functions, and see which one always gives the corresponding value in the chart. If we plug $x = 3$ into choice **A**, we get 12; but when we plug in $x = 4$, we don't get 19. So we can eliminate choice **A**. If we plug $x = 3$ into choice **B**, we get 12; if we plug in $x = 4$, we get 19; if we plug in $x = 5$, we get 28; and if we plug in $x = 6$ we get 39. Therefore, **B** is the answer.

You won't always see a problem written with the symbol $f(x)$, but any problem of this type is still a function problem and can be solved the same way. Here's an example:

Shirts	Free Gifts
5	15
6	17
7	19
8	21

For its grand opening, a store is giving away free gifts to customers who buy shirts, according to the table above. If s is the number of shirts that a customer buys, which of the following shows the number of gifts that customer will receive?

A. $2s$

B. $3s$

C. $2s + 5$

D. $4s - 5$

Once again, we need to plug into each answer choice the values for s from the left-hand side of the table and see which one gives us the results that appear on the right-hand side of the table. Let's start with **A**. If $s=5$, then $2s = 10$, so we can eliminate **A**. How about **B**? If $s = 5$, then $3s = 15$; if $s = 6$, then $3s = 18$. This eliminates **B**. So let's move on to **C**. If $s = 5$, then $2s + 5 = 15$; if $s = 6$, then $2s + 5 = 17$; if $s = 7$, then $2s + 5 = 19$; if $s = 8$, then $2s + 5 = 21$. This works for each one of the entries, so choice **C** is the answer.

Plug In whenever you see variables!

Range and domain

The *range* of a function is all of the possible results of a function. The *domain* of a function is all the values of x that you can put into it. Take a look at the following:

> What is the range, in integers, of the function $f(x) = x^2$
>
> A. All integers greater than 0
>
> B. All integers greater than -1
>
> C. All integers between 0 and 100
>
> D. All even integers

This question is, in effect, asking us to figure out what numbers might result from this function. To figure this out, let's try plugging in several values for x. A good sample would be the numbers from -3 to 3 along with a very large negative number and a very large positive number. We can put the results into a table:

x	-10	-3	-2	-1	0	1	2	3	10
$f(x)$	100	9	4	1	0	1	4	9	100

Plugging In never fails!

Since we can get 0 and 9 from this function, we know that the range does include 0 and odd integers, so we can eliminate choices **A** and **D**. If we were to plug in a larger number for x, we could also get a result that is larger than 100, so we can eliminate choice **C** as well. This leaves **B** as the best answer.

Minimum or maximum values

Another kind of function problem may ask you for *minimum* or *maximum* values of a function. Here's an example:

> For which of the following values of x will the function $f(x) = 10 - x^2$ have the greatest value?
>
> A. $x = 10$
>
> B. $x = 5$
>
> C. $x = -10$
>
> D. $x = 1$

PATTERNS, RELATIONS, AND FUNCTIONS

If we plug into the function each of these values for x, what happens to the function? If $x = 10$, the result is -90. If $x = 5$, the result is -15. If $x = 10$, the result is -90, and if $x = 1$, the result is 9. Therefore, **D** is the answer.

Changing the values

Finally, another kind of function question may ask you what happens to a function when you change one of its variables:

In the formula $x = \dfrac{1}{y^2}$, if the value of y (given that y is not 0) is doubled, the value of x becomes:

A. twice as large

B. four times as large

C. $\dfrac{1}{2}$ as large

D. $\dfrac{1}{4}$ as large

> Plugging In is the way to go on function problems!

The way to solve this kind of question is to plug in one value for y, double it, and plug it in again. Let's try $y = 2$. This makes $x = \dfrac{1}{4}$. Now if we double the value of y, making $y = 4$, the value of x becomes $\dfrac{1}{16}$. Since x has gone from $\dfrac{1}{4}$ to $\dfrac{1}{16}$, it has become one-fourth as large, so the answer is **D**.

Graphs and Charts

The MCAS exam writers are very fond of problems involving graphs, so you'll probably see several of them. Graphs are a way of visualizing functions by placing them on the coordinate plane. The basic line functions we discussed in the last chapter (for instance, ones that take the form $y = 3x + 5$) are good examples.

One of the skills you will need to master is predicting how a graph will look from a set of points. You can do this by plotting the points, but it can also be done by looking at the points and figuring out their pattern.

1	2	3	4	5	6	7
100	200	300	400	500	600	700
100	150	175	185	190	193	194
100	200	300	400	300	200	100
100	150	160	165	160	150	100

Above are the points for four different graphs. To get an idea of how each one looks, let's take its points and write down the difference between every two points:

1	2	3	4	5	6	7
100 (+ 100)	200 (+ 100)	300 (+ 100)	400 (+ 100)	500 (+ 100)	600 (+ 100)	700
100 (+ 50)	150 (+ 25)	175 (+ 10)	185 (+ 5)	190 (+ 3)	193 (+ 1)	194
100 (+ 100)	200 (+ 100)	300 (+ 100)	400 (− 100)	300 (− 100)	200 (− 100)	100
100 (+ 50)	150 (+ 10)	160 (+ 5)	165 (− 5)	160 (− 50)	150 (− 50)	100

The first series of points goes up at a steady pace: Each number is 100 larger than the number before it. Therefore, it will go up in a nice straight line, as in figure **A** below. The second series goes up, but it goes up at a slower and slower rate as the line moves. This means that it will look something like figure **C** below. The third series goes up at a steady rate and then goes down at a steady rate. So it will look like figure **B** below. The last series begins by going up quickly, then going up more slowly, then going down slowly, and ends by going down quickly. It will look something like figure **D** below.

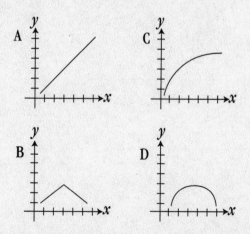

PATTERNS, RELATIONS, AND FUNCTIONS

Now try the following problem:

Number of Engines	1	2	3	4	5
Speed	50	81	110	140	172

Which graph best represents the relationship between the number of engines and the speed of the rocket?

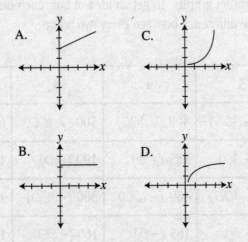

A.

C.

B.

D.

Sometimes all you have to do is notice a pattern in the numbers on the graph.

If we look at the pattern in the speeds above, we see that each number is about 30 more than the number before it. This means that the graph will look like a straight line that gradually goes upwards from 50. This makes **A** the best choice.

Reading a chart

One variation on chart problems requires you to read information off of a chart that may not exactly be designed for ease of reading.

Here's an example:

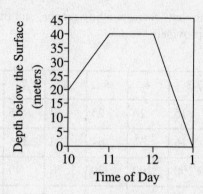

The graph above shows the depth of a diver below the surface of a lake. Which of the following best fits the information shown in the chart?

A. The diver begins at the surface of the lake, swims down to the top of an underwater rock, and then swims back up to the surface.

B. The diver begins at the bottom of the lake, swims up to the top of an underwater rock, and then swims down to the bottom again.

C. The diver begins on top of an underwater rock, swims up to the surface of the lake, and then swims down to the bottom of the lake.

D. The diver begins on top of an underwater rock, swims down to the bottom of the lake, and then swims up to the surface of the lake.

> Make sure you read graphs and charts *very* carefully.

The challenge in this problem is to read the chart very carefully, especially the axes. In this case, the *y*-axis shows the depth of the diver, so the higher the line, the deeper the diver must be. We can see that at the beginning, the depth of the diver increases. This means that the diver first goes *down*. This will allow us to eliminate **B** and **C**. Since the diver begins partway down, we can also eliminate **A**. This leaves **D** as the best choice.

Here are a few problems to help practice what we've just covered.

Exercise 5 (answers on page 123)

Translate the following into algebra:

a. Half the value of x is equal to 6 times the difference between 24 and 12.

b. 78 is less than twice the product of x and 18.

c. $\frac{1}{5}$ of the difference between 6 and x is equal to twice the product of y and 5.

d. Factor: $x^2 + 3x - 10$

e   If $x^2 + 15x + 50 = 0$, what are the possible values of x?

Match the following series with their corresponding graphs, and fill in the letter of the corresponding graph on the blanks provided:

	1	2	3	4	5	6	7	Graph:
f.	5	10	15	20	25	30	35	
g.	4	8	16	32	64	128	256	
h.	40	70	90	100	90	70	40	
i.	110	105	95	80	60	35	5	
j.	500	200	100	60	45	35	30	

A.
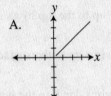

C.
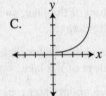

B.
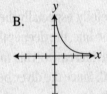

D.
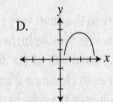

E.
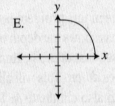

k.   In the function $f(x) = 3x - 5$, what is the value of the function when x is 0? When x is 5?

The following table shows the number of bacteria over a 25-hour period.

Time (hrs)	Number of bacteria
0	750
5	11,000
10	44,000
15	35,000
20	11,000
25	6,000

1   Which of the following graphs best represents the results shown in the table above?

A.
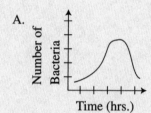

C.
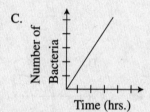

B.
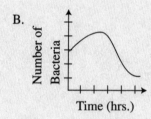

D.
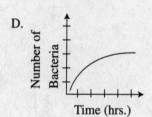

2   Which of the following functions will be positive for $x = -10$?

A. $f(x) = 2x + x^1$

B. $f(x) = 3x + x^2$

C. $f(x) = 5x - 20$

D. $f(x) = -x - 10$

Side	Area
1	1
2	4
3	9
4	16

3   Which graph best represents the relationship between the side of a square and its area?

A.
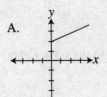

C.
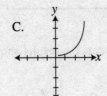

B.
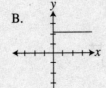

D.
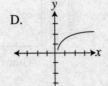

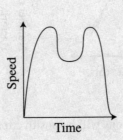

4   The graph above shows the speed of a bicyclist going home from school. Which of the following best fits the information shown in the chart?

A. The bicyclist begins by riding slowly uphill, speeds up while going downhill, and then slows down to climb uphill to her house, where she stops.

B. The bicyclist begins by riding quickly downhill, slows down while going uphill, and then speeds up again before reaching her house, where she stops.

C. The bicyclist begins by riding quickly downhill, and then slows down gradually as she approaches her house, where she stops.

D. The bicyclist begins by riding slowly uphill, and then gradually picks up speed as she rides downhill to her house, where she stops.

5   If x is 4 more than twice the difference between y and 3, which of the following expresses the relationship of x and y?

A. $x = 4 + (y - 3)$

B. $x = 2 + 4 (y - 3)$

C. $x = 4 + 2(y - 3)$

D. $x + 4 = 2(y - 3)$

Chapter 6

Statistics and Probability

Statistics and probability questions deal with different ways of interpreting information. The calculations required for these kinds of problems usually aren't too complicated. However, knowing how to set up the problem can be a bit tricky.

Sampling and Proportions

You will probably encounter one or two questions on the MCAS exam that give you information about a sample of items in a group, and ask you to draw conclusions about the whole group. The way to solve these is by setting up a proportion.

For instance, let's say we know that of a sample of 10 students in a school, 3 are boys. We can write this as the fraction $\frac{3}{10}$. Of course, if we say that out of every 10 students, 3 are boys, this doesn't tell us exactly how many students we have. But if our sample is accurate, and if we know the total number of students, we can always solve for the number of boys in the total population. For example, if there are 20 students, there should be 6 boys; if there are 100 students, there should be 30 boys, and so on. With easy proportions, you can probably do this kind of work in your head. But it's always better to play it safe and do the work on paper. So we have to know how to reliably set up and calculate proportions. Let's take a look to see how we do that.

Setting up a proportion

The way to solve sampling questions is to set up two fractions and cross-multiply:

$$\frac{A}{B} = \frac{C}{D}$$

> Proportions are the key to sampling questions.

Whenever you set up two equal fractions, you know that $A \times D$ is equal to $C \times B$. In order for the fractions to be equal, the numbers on the tops of the two fractions must represent values/amounts from the same group/category, as must the numbers on the bottom of the fractions.

In this case, if we know that 3 of every 10 students are boys, and that there are 200 students, we can figure out the number of boys by setting up these fractions:

$$\frac{\text{Boys}}{\text{Total Students}} = \frac{3}{10} = \frac{x}{200}$$

Now we can cross-multiply: $10x = 3 \times 200$. This means that $x = 60$.

Let's try the following problem:

> Alex found 5 pounds of peanuts in a 23-pound bag of candy. Approximately how many pounds of peanuts would you expect to find in 105 pounds of the same candy?
>
> A. 18 pounds
>
> B. 22 pounds
>
> C. 29 pounds
>
> D. 32 pounds

To solve this, set up a proportion:

$$\frac{\text{Peanuts}}{\text{All Candy}} = \frac{5}{23} = \frac{x}{105}$$

Now we can cross-multiply: $23x = 5 \times 105$, so $x =$ about 22 pounds, choice **B**.

Note that proportions also work with geometry:

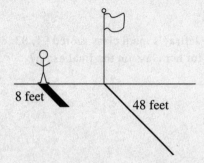

8 feet

48 feet

Kimberly wants to figure out the height of a tall flagpole at her school. At a certain time of day, Kimberly's shadow is 8 feet long, and the shadow of the flagpole is 48 feet long. If Kimberly is 5 feet tall, how tall is the flagpole?

A. 25 feet

B. 28 feet

C. 30 feet

D. 45 feet

In this case we can set up a proportion between Kimberly's height and Kimberly's shadow, which we can then apply to the flagpole's height and the flagpole's shadow:

$$\frac{\text{Height}}{\text{Shadow}} = \frac{5}{8} = \frac{x}{48}$$

If we cross-multiply and solve for x, we find that $8x = 240$. Therefore, $x = 30$ feet, making the correct answer choice **C**.

Mean, Median, Mode, and Range

The *mean*, the *median*, and the *mode* are three different ways of taking the average of a group of numbers.

> **Remember:** The mean is equal to the total divided by the number of things.

Mean

The *mean* is probably what you normally think of when you think of averages.

$$\text{Mean} = \frac{\text{total}}{\# \text{ of things}}$$

If a student's test scores are 60, 65, and 75, the mean for those tests = $\frac{60 + 65 + 75}{3} = 66.67$.

Try the following problem:

If the 5 students in Ms. Jaffray's math class scored 91, 83, 84, 90, and 85 on their final exams, what is the mean score for her class on the final exam?

To figure out the mean, we calculate

$$\frac{91+83+84+90+85}{5} = \frac{433}{5} = 86.6$$

Notice that you can also figure out the total if you know the mean and the number of things. For instance, if a student had a mean score of 50 on 3 tests, her total score can be calculated, since the mean of $50 = \frac{\text{total}}{3}$. Therefore her total score on her 3 tests must be 150. This can be useful in more complex average problems in which you have to find the total. Here's an example:

If the 5 students in Ms. Jaffray's math class had a mean score of 80 on the final exam, and if 4 of the students scored 85, what did the fifth student score?

In this case, we know that 5 students have a mean score of 80. This will allow us to calculate the total number of points that the 5 students must have had. We know that $80 = \frac{\text{Total}}{5}$, so we can figure out that the total score for all 5 students must have been 400. Now we also know that four of the students scored 85, so we can figure out that they account for 85 + 85 + 85 + 85 = 340 of those 400 total points. This means that the remaining student scored a 60.

Median

The *median* of a group of numbers is the number in the middle (just as the median is the large divider in the middle of a road).

First, line up the elements in the group in numerical order, from lowest to highest. If the number of elements in your group is *odd*, find the number in the middle. That's the median.

If the 5 students in Ms. Jaffray's math class scored 91, 83, 84, 90, and 85 on their final exams, what is the median score for her class on the final exam?

Remember: The median is the middle number.

First, let's place these numbers in order from lowest to highest: 83, 84, 85, 90, 91. The number in the middle is 85, so the median of this group is 85.

But what if you have an *even* number of elements in the group? Find the two numbers in the middle and calculate their mean.

If the 6 students in Ms. Jaffray's math class scored 91, 83, 84, 90, 92, and 85, and on their final exams, what is the median score for her class on the final exam?

When we place these numbers in order, we get 83, 84, 85, 90, 91, and 92. Since the numbers in the middle are 85 and 90, we take their mean, which is 87.5.

Mode

The *mode* of a group of numbers is the number that appears the most.

Try this problem:

Remember: Mode = The number that appears the most.

If the 7 students in Ms. Jaffray's math class scored 91, 83, 92, 83, 91, 85, and 91 on their final exams, what is the mode of her students' scores?

If we place these numbers in order, we get: 83, 83, 85, 91, 91, 91, and 92. Since the number 91 is the one that appears most often in the list, the mode of these numbers is 91.

The following set of numbers represents the results (in inches) from Allison's five frogs in a recent frog-jumping contest:

{10.8, 11.1, 9.5, 11.1, 12}

Which of the following sets represents the average, median, and mode, respectively, for the results of Allison's five frogs in the frog-jumping contest?

A. {10.8, 9.5, 10.8}

B. {10.8, 9.5, 11.1}

C. {10.9, 11.1, 11.1}

D. {10.9, 11.1, 12}

To find the average, just add up the numbers and divide by 5 (the number of elements in the set.) That gives us $10.8 + 11.1 + 9.5 + 11.1 + 12 \div 5 = 54.5 \div 5 = 10.9$ as our average. The mode is the number that appears most often, which is 11.1, as it occurs twice (that's once more than any other number in the set). Finally, when we list the numbers in order, {9.5, 10.8, 11.1, 11.1, 12}, we find that 11.1 falls directly in the middle. Answer choice **C** puts these values in their correct order, making it the right answer.

Range

The *range* of a group of numbers is the difference between the largest and the smallest elements in the group. It shows over how big a stretch the numbers extend, from the lowest to the highest value.

For example, for the group 44, 11, 23, 31, 7, we take the difference between the largest value, 44, and the smallest value, 7. The range of this group is $44 - 7$, or 37.

> The range is the difference between the largest and smallest numbers in a group.

Graphing Data

One to three problems on the Grade 10 Math MCAS exam will ask you to read data points from a graph or to plot data points on a graph.

Line of best fit

You may be asked to plot a set of points on a chart and draw a *line of best fit*. A line of best fit is essentially the line you would get if you averaged all the points on the graph and charted the results. That is, it separates all of the points evenly. Here's an example of a series of points and a best-fit line.

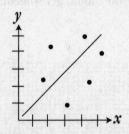

You probably won't be given enough information to calculate the exact placement of the line, but if your line passes roughly through the center of the data points, you should get full credit for the answer.

When you're creating a line of best fit, try to have the same number of points on either side of the line. The graph above has three points on either side of the line of best fit, so you know that it's accurate.

Now try the following problem:

Plot the following points on the grid provided, and draw a single straight line that best represents the data. (1, 2) (2, 3) (3, 0) (4, 3) (5, 1) (6, 5) (7, 2)

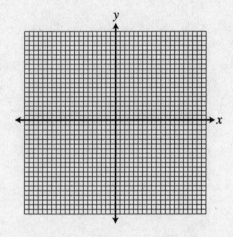

Which of the following lines could be the line of best fit for the data points above?

A. $y = -2x$

B. $y = 2x + 8$

C. $y = \frac{1}{2}x$

D. $y = \frac{1}{2}x + 5$

If you plot your points accurately, you should get something like this:

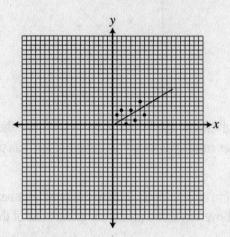

Now let's use POE. Because the line goes up and to the right, it must have a positive slope, so we can eliminate choice **A**. By estimating we can see that the line is shallower than a 45-degree angle, so the slope will be less than 1. This will allow us to eliminate **B**. Finally, the *y*-intercept could not be as large as 5, so we can eliminate **D**. This leaves **C** as our best answer.

Interpolation

Don't worry; you don't have to remember what this word means. You only have to remember how to do it. *Interpolation* means figuring out the value of a point on a chart even though that point is not exactly on one of the grid lines. You can figure out approximately what the value of that point should be by looking at the grid lines that it is closest to, and estimating.

> To interpolate is to figure out the value of a point on a chart, even if that point is not exactly on one of the grid lines.

Try this with the following graph:

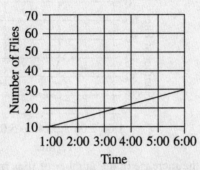

The chart above shows the increase in the number of flies in a jar over the course of an afternoon. About how many flies were there at 5:30 PM?

A. 17

B. 20

C. 25

D. 29

Although there's no grid line at 5:30, we can see that at 5:00 there were about 25 flies, and at 6:00 there were about 30 flies, so we can estimate that there were about 28 or 29 flies at 5:30. This will eliminate **A** and **B**. Choice **C** isn't quite as close a choice as **D**, so **D** is the best answer.

Extrapolation

Here's another word you don't have to know. You simply have to be able to follow a trend. *Extrapolation* just means extending a line farther than is shown on the graph. If you are ever asked to extrapolate, remember: Keep following the general shape of the line. If the line is straight, you should continue drawing a straight line at the same angle. If the line curves, follow the same curve.

> To extrapolate, simply follow the general shape of the line!

Here's an example:

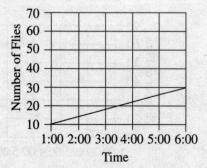

The chart above shows the increase in the number of flies in a jar over the course of an afternoon. If the trend on the chart does not change, about how many flies will there be at 8:00 PM?

A. 30

B. 40

C. 50

D. 60

In this case, the trend follows a nice straight line, so let's just extend that line out a little farther and see where it lands. If you take the edge of your formula sheet and place it against the line, you'll see that 2 hours later, the line will land at about 40. You can also see that the number of flies increases by about 10 every 2 hours, too. That's choice **B**.

Now let's try a slightly harder problem:

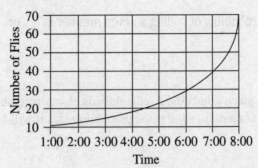

The chart above shows the increase in the number of flies in a jar over the course of an afternoon. If the trend shown on the chart does not change, about how many flies will there be at 9:00 PM?

A. 75

B. 85

C. 120

D. 190

If we look at the last hour on the chart, the hour from 7:00–8:00, we can see that the number of flies increases from 40 to 70, an increase of 30 in an hour. We can also see that the rate has been increasing over time (there were only 10 more flies from 6:00 to 7:00), so in the next hour, the number of flies should increase by more than 30. That eliminates **A** and **B**. If there are 70 flies at 8:00, there will probably be a little more than 100 by 8:00. This makes choice **C** the best answer.

Probability

Probability refers to the chance that an event will happen, and is always given as a fraction between 0 and 1. A probability of 0 means that the event will never happen; a probability of 1 means that it is certain to happen.

> **Remember:** Probability is equal to the number of outcomes you want divided by the number of possible outcomes.

$$\text{Probability} = \frac{\text{Number of Outcomes You Want}}{\text{Number of Possible Outcomes}}$$

For instance, if you have a number cube with faces numbered 1 to 6, what is the chance of rolling a 2? There is one face with the number 2 on it, out of 6 total faces. Therefore, the probability of rolling a 2 is $\frac{1}{6}$.

What is the chance of rolling an even number on one roll of this number cube? There are 3 faces of the cube with an even number (the sides numbered 2, 4, and 6) out of a total of 6 faces. Therefore, the probability of rolling an even number is $\frac{3}{6}$, or $\frac{1}{2}$.

Try one:

In a jar there are 3 green gumballs, 5 red gumballs, 8 white gumballs, and 1 blue gumball. If 1 gumball is chosen at random, what is the probability that it will be red?

A. $\frac{5}{17}$

B. $\frac{5}{16}$

C. $\frac{1}{17}$

D. $\frac{1}{12}$

To solve this problem, we take the number of things we want (the 5 red gumballs) and place it over the number of possible things we have to choose from (all 17 gumballs in the jar). This gives us choice **A**.

Probability of individual events

The probability that two events will both happen is always the product of the probabilities of the individual events. For instance, if we flip a coin, the probability that it will land on "heads" is $\frac{1}{2}$. What is the chance that on two flips, the coin will land on "heads" twice in a row?

First flip	Second flip	Probability
$\frac{1}{2}$ $\times$	$\frac{1}{2}$ =	$\frac{1}{4}$

On the first flip, the chance of the coin landing on "heads" is $\frac{1}{2}$. On the second flip, the chance of the coin landing on "heads" is also $\frac{1}{2}$. So the chance that it will land on "heads" twice in a row is $\frac{1}{4}$.

Now try this problem:

> If you roll 2 number cubes, each with faces numbered 1 to 6, what is the probability that you will roll 2 sixes?
>
> A. $\dfrac{1}{6}$
>
> B. $\dfrac{2}{6}$
>
> C. $\dfrac{1}{18}$
>
> D. $\dfrac{1}{36}$

We need to find the probability of the individual events, and then find their product. On the first cube, the chance of rolling a 6 is $\dfrac{1}{6}$. On the second cube, the chance of rolling a 6 is $\dfrac{1}{6}$.

So the chance of rolling 2 sixes is $\left(\dfrac{1}{6}\right)\left(\dfrac{1}{6}\right)$, or $\dfrac{1}{36}$. That's choice **D**.

Probability of multiple independent events

What if you have to find the probability of two independent events?

> If you roll 2 number cubes, each with faces numbered 1 to 6, what is the probability that the sum of the numbers will be 7?

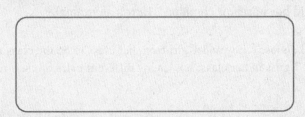

In this case, we don't have two different events, so we can't just take the product of the probabilities of the individual events. Instead, we need to figure out in how many cases the sum of 2 cubes will be 7, and in how many cases the sum of the 2 cubes will not be 7.

The easiest way to solve this is to make a sample space and draw out all the possibilities:

	1	2	3	4	5	6
1	2	3	4	5	6	7
2	3	4	5	6	7	8
3	4	5	6	7	8	9
4	5	6	7	8	9	10
5	6	7	8	9	10	11
6	7	8	9	10	11	12

Across the top of the chart we have the number rolled on 1 cube; down the side we have the number rolled on the other. In the middle are the sums of the numbers rolled on each cube. In how many cases is the sum equal to 7? In 6 cases. So there are 6 ways to get a sum of 7. How many total numbers is it possible to get? 36. So the chance that the sum of the two cubes will equal 7 is $\frac{6}{36}$, or $\frac{1}{6}$.

Combinations

Combination problems ask you how many different ways a number of things could be chosen or combined. Here's an example:

Ms. Grady will choose 1 boy and 1 girl from her class to be the class representatives. If there are 3 boys and 7 girls in her class, how many different pairs of class representatives could she pick?

A. 10

B. 13

C. 21

D. 23

There's a very simple rule for combination problems:

> The number of combinations is the product of the number of things you have to choose from.

In the problem above, Ms. Grady has 3 boys to choose from and 7 girls to choose from, so the number of different combinations she could choose is 3 × 7, or 21.

Don't forget to watch out for certain cases where some of the choices are fixed and, therefore, don't actually count as choices. Here's an example:

Students at Smalltown High

Eighth Grade	9
Ninth Grade	8
Tenth Grade	10

Mr. Livingstone will choose 1 eighth-grader, 1 ninth-grader, and 1 tenth-grader from the students at Smalltown High to be on the student council. If he knows that the ninth-grader on the student council will be Julia Witherspoon, how many different combinations of students could he pick for the student council?

A. 72

B. 80

C. 90

D. 720

Though the problem begins by saying there are 8 ninth-graders, it turns out that there is only 1 possibility for the ninth-grader. The number of ninth-graders that Mr. Livingstone can choose from is, in fact, only 1. So the correct way to figure out the number of possible combinations is to multiply.

Eighth-grade	×	Ninth-grade	×	Tenth-grade
9	×	1	×	10

The product is 90, so the answer is **C**.

Now that you've mastered these topics, try the following problems.

a. If a student scores 60, 70, 95, and 105, what is the mean score for these tests?

b. If a student has a mean score of 75 on 5 tests, what is the total of the scores received on those tests?

c. The mean of 4 numbers is 80. If 2 of the numbers are 50 and 60, what is the sum of the other 2 numbers?

d. What is the median of this group of numbers:

    44, 11, 23, 31, and 7?

    How about this one:

    25, 12, 34, 28, 21, 29?

e. What is the mode of this group of numbers: 6, 8, 11, 65, 8, 11, 24, and 8?

f. In a group of 100 residents of City X, 18 had blond hair. If City X has 250,000 residents, about how many people would you expect to have blond hair ?

1   In an 8-pound bag of trail mix, there are 3 pounds of raisins. If this sample is accurate, approximately how many pounds of raisins would you expect to find in 135 pounds of trail mix?

    A. 24 pounds

    B. 35 pounds

    C. 45 pounds

    D. 50 pounds

2   For which of the following groups is the median equal to the mode?

    A. 15, 19, 54, 15, 22

    B. 26, 32, 18, 26, 15, 28

    C. 32, 19, 28, 16, 19, 25

    D. 33, 18, 19, 13, 18

Ice Cream	Toppings
Chocolate	Peanuts
Vanilla	Hot Fudge
Strawberry	Chocolate Chips
Wild Berry	
Coffee	

3   Kim is going to buy an ice cream sundae. A sundae consists of 1 flavor of ice cream and 1 topping. If she can choose from the kinds of ice cream and toppings above, how many different sundaes could she create?

A. 8

B. 12

C. 15

D. 18

4   At the school cafeteria, students can choose from 3 different salads, 5 different main dishes, and 2 different desserts. If Isabel chooses 1 salad, 1 main dish, and 1 dessert for lunch, how many different lunches could she choose?

A. 15

B. 30

C. 45

D. 60

5   If a drawer contains 6 white socks, 6 black socks, and 8 red socks, what is the probability that a sock drawn at random from the drawer will be red?

A. $\frac{1}{8}$

B. $\frac{2}{5}$

C. $\frac{1}{2}$

D. $\frac{2}{3}$

6   A bowl of marbles contains 8 blue marbles, 6 green marbles, 10 red marbles, and 1 white marble. If 1 marble is drawn at random from the bowl, what is the probability that it will be either blue or green?

A. $\dfrac{8}{25}$

B. $\dfrac{9}{25}$

C. $\dfrac{14}{25}$

D. $\dfrac{4}{5}$

7   John is choosing an outfit to wear to school. He will choose 1 shirt, 1 pair of pants, and 1 pair of socks. If he has 5 shirts, 4 pairs of pants, and 8 pairs of socks to choose from, how many different outfits could John choose?

Fruits sold at the fruit stand

Bananas	8
Apples	25
Pears	13
Oranges	8
Pineapples	6

8 The table above shows the number of pieces of various kinds of fruit sold at the fruit stand on a given day. What is the chance that the next piece of fruit sold will be an orange?

A. $\dfrac{1}{10}$

B. $\dfrac{2}{15}$

C. $\dfrac{4}{15}$

D. $\dfrac{4}{25}$

9a. Plot the following points on the grid provided and draw a single straight line that best represents the data.

x	y
-1	2
-2	6
-3	3
-4	10
-5	7

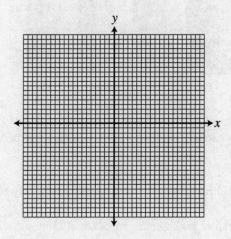

b. What could be the slope of the line of best fit that you drew?

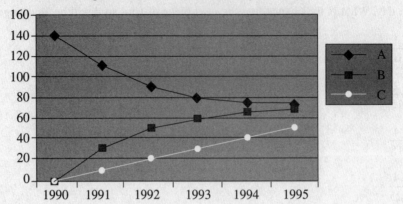

10 The chart above shows the number of hammers sold at stores A, B, and C from the years 1990–1995.

a. About how many hammers were sold in store A in 1994?

b. Which store will probably sell the most hammers in 1998? Explain your answer.

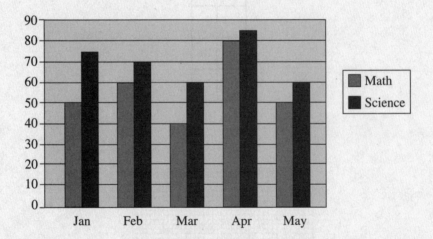

11 The chart above shows John's math and science scores for the monthly tests he took in the first 5 months of the year.

a. In which month did John have the greatest difference between his math and science scores?

b. What was the mean of his science scores for all 5 months?

c. What was the range of his math scores for all 5 months?

Final Thoughts

Tests and practice

What follows are the answers to the previous drills and the sample tests and an example of the formula sheet you'll be provided with on test day. When taking the practice tests, remember that you won't be allowed to use your calculator during the first session. You should also have the formula sheet handy, so you can get used to using it. (We suggest that you photocopy the formula sheet rather than tearing it out of the book. This will make it easier for you to use while you're taking your test. If you're in a really bad mood, and it would make you feel better, feel free to mangle this book, as long as it's your copy and doesn't belong to your library or your friend.)

Remember that when you practice, the number of problems you get right or wrong is less important than knowing *why* you got a problem right or wrong. When you find yourself in trouble on a certain problem, look back to the pages that cover that topic, or ask a teacher or a friend for help. Taking these tests may not be a lot of fun, but as with any skill, you can improve with practice.

On your test days

Remember to prepare mentally for these tests. Be sure to be well rested and well fed. Be sure you've got everything you need—especially your calculator on the days you're allowed to use it. (Remember that you'll be provided with one if you forget yours, but it's always better to use the one with which you're familiar and comfortable.) Think happy thoughts. And remember that it's only a test.

Chapter 7

Solutions to Exercises

Exercise 3.1

a. $\dfrac{46}{1000}$ or $\dfrac{23}{500}$

b. $\dfrac{3}{5}$ is the same as $\dfrac{6}{10}$, which is .6

c. $\dfrac{2}{50}$ is the same as $\dfrac{4}{100}$, which equals .04

d. Anything to the 0 power equals 1, and anything to the first power is itself, so this becomes 1 times 18, or 18.

e. Anything to the 0 power equals 1, so this becomes the square root of 1, which is 1.

1 C Choices **B** and **D** are integers, so they can be eliminated. Choice **A** is not rational, so it can also be eliminated. This leaves us with **C**.

2 C To solve this problem, try plugging in a negative odd integer and a positive even integer. -3 times 4 gives us -12, which is negative and even. Therefore, **C** is the best answer.

3 B $\dfrac{1}{50}$ is equal to .02, and $\dfrac{4}{20}$ is equal to .2, so we are looking for a number between .02 and 2. Choice **A** is smaller than .02, so we can cross it off. Choices **C** and **D** are bigger than .2, so they can also be eliminated. This leaves us with **B**.

4 C Remember that to the right of the decimal point, the digits closest to the decimal are the largest. Since it has a 0 in the tenths place, choice **A** is smaller than .338. Choice **B** is also smaller since it has the same numbers in the tenths and hundredths place, and nothing in the thousandths place. Choice **C** has a 4 in the hundredths place, which is larger than the 3 in .338.

5 A The easiest way to solve this problem is to convert the fractions to decimals. Choice **A** has $\dfrac{3}{5}$ and $\dfrac{4}{5}$, which in decimal form become .6 and .8. Since .71 is between .6 and .8, choice **A** is the answer.

6 B Remember that a negative number raised to an even power will become positive, while a negative number raised to an odd power will stay negative. We know that choice **A** will be negative, while choice **B** becomes positive. Choices **C** and **D** are also positive, but **B** has a larger base and a larger exponent, so choice **B** must be the largest.

7 B Let's plug in $\dfrac{1}{2}$ for x in these choices and see which is largest. Choice **A** becomes 2.5, **B** becomes 10, and **C** becomes $\dfrac{1}{10}$. Do we even need to calculate choice **D**? We know that a fraction raised to a power gets smaller, so we know that **D** will be smaller than $\dfrac{1}{2}$.

8 A Let's try plugging in $\dfrac{1}{4}$. In A, $\left(\dfrac{1}{4}\right)^2 = \dfrac{1}{16}$, which is smaller than $\dfrac{1}{4}$. $\sqrt{\dfrac{1}{4}} = \dfrac{1}{2}$, which is larger than $\dfrac{1}{4}$. Since $\dfrac{1}{16} < \dfrac{1}{4}$ and $\dfrac{1}{4} < \dfrac{1}{2}$, we know that $y^2 < y < \sqrt{y}$.

9 D Let's try plugging in some easy numbers. If x is -5 and y is 4, then their product will be -20. This will eliminate choices **A**, **B**, and **C**. This makes **D** the best choice.

Exercise 3.2

a. $4x + 3 = 31$. The first step is to subtract 3 from each side, which gives us $4x = 28$. Now we can divide each side by 4, to get $x = 7$.

b. $5x - 4 = 3x$. Let's subtract $3x$ from each side to get all the xs on the left side of the equation. This gives us $2x - 4 = 0$. Now let's add 4 to each side, which gives us $2x = 4$. When we divide each side by 2, we get $x = 2$.

c. $5x - 4 > 4x$. If we subtract $4x$ from each side, we get $x - 4 > 0$. Now we add 4 to each side and get $x > 4$. Since we did not multiply or divide by a negative value, there was no need to change the direction of the inequality.

d. The percent increase will be equal to $\dfrac{4,000}{20,000}$, which is $\dfrac{1}{5}$, or 20%.

e. Let's plug in a number for the price of the car. If the car is $100, and its price increases by 30%, it will increase by $30 to $130 in the first year. In the second year it will increase 30% of $130, which is an increase of $39 to $169. So in 2 years it has increased from $100 to $169, which is a 69% increase.

f. Translate "20% of 420" as: $\dfrac{20}{100} \times 420 = 84$.

g. Translate "15 equals 30% of what number" as: $15 = \dfrac{30}{100}x$, so $x = 50$.

h. The increase from $80 to $100 is an increase of $20. This over the original price gives us $\dfrac{20}{80}$, which is the same as $\dfrac{1}{4}$, or 25%.

i. If we increase the 1990 price of the coin by 10%, we get 10% of $120, or $12. The price of the coin in 1991 was $132.

j. Let's keep increasing the price. From 1991 to 1992, the price increased by 10% of $132, or $13.20, to a new price of $145.20. From 1992 to 1993, the price increased by 10% of $145.20, or $14.52, to a new price of $159.72. From 1993 to 1994, the price increased by 10% of $159.72, or $15.97, to a new price of $175.69.

k. Let's keep increasing by 10%. By 1995, it increased by 10% of $175.69, or $17.57, to a new price of $193.26. By 1996, then, the coin cost more than $200.

1 **C** We can find the percent decrease by taking the amount of change in the population and dividing it by the original population. $\frac{400}{1200} = \frac{1}{3} =$ a 33% decrease.

2 **D** Let's read the chart and figure out how many employees took a vacation in the months of August, September, and October. In August, 10 employees took a vacation; in September, 20 employees; in October, about 3 employees. That makes a total of 33 employees out of the total of 80 employees. 33 is what percent of 80? We can translate this question as:

$33 = \frac{x}{100} \times 80$. If we solve for x, we get $x = 41.25\%$, or about 40%.

3 **C** It looks like Y and Z combined make less than half, but more than a quarter, of the circle. If there are 600 people voting, the number who vote for Y and Z should be more than one-quarter (150) and less than one-half (300) of the people. This will allow us to eliminate choices **A** and **D**. In fact, Y and Z together make up a lot more than a quarter of the circle, so the answer is **C**.

4 **B** From the chart we can see that Sarah sold more magazines than books, but not twice as many. If she sold 350 books, she must have sold more than 350 magazines, but not as many as 700. This will allow us to eliminate **A** and **D**. Looking closer, it seems that the number of magazines is nowhere near twice as large as the number of books, and choice **C** is just very close to 700. So the best answer is **B**.

5 ***Remember***: The percent increase is equal to the amount of change over the original amount. Store A had an increase of 45 over the original 80; store B had an increase of 45 over the original 25. This means that the percent increase for store A was $\frac{45}{80}$, which is a little more than $\frac{1}{2}$, or 50%. The percent increase for store B was $\frac{45}{20}$, which is slightly more than 200%. So store B had a larger percent increase.

Exercise 4.1

a. The third side of the triangle has to be big enough so that the sum of it and 9 is larger than 11. Since all the sides are integer values, the smallest that the third side could be is 3, since $9 + 3 > 11$. Therefore, the smallest perimeter of the triangle is $9 + 11 + 3$, or 23.

b. The third side of the triangle has to be small enough so that it is not bigger than the sum of $9 + 11$. So the biggest that the third side could be is 19. This makes the perimeter of the triangle $9 + 11 + 19$, or 39.

c. We know that one of the sides of the rectangle is the line from $(2, 5)$ to $(2, -4)$. This is a length of 9. One other side of the rectangle is the line from $(-3, -4)$ to $(2, -4)$, which has a length of 5. Therefore, the area of the rectangle is 9×5, or 45 sq. units.

d. In the given rectangle, we have sides 6 and 10. Since we know that in any rectangle, the opposite sides are equal, x must be 10 and y must be 6. But be careful! The question asks for the sum $x + y$, which is $10 + 6$, or 16.

e. Since this circle has a radius of 7, its area is πr^2, or 49π sq. units. Its circumference is $2\pi r$, or 14π units. In 1 revolution, it will travel a distance equal to its circumference, so in 10 revolutions it will travel $10 \times 14\pi$, which is 140π units.

1 C Let's write down everything we know about this triangle. The angle next to the 55-degree angle must be 125 degrees because there are 180 degrees on a line. If that angle is 125 degrees, and $y = 35$ degrees, then we have a total of 160 degrees in the triangle that contains angle x. Since the number of angles in the triangle must be 180 degrees, we know that $x = 20$ degrees. This makes **C** the answer.

2 A The figures in choice **C** are similar, but they are also congruent since they are exactly the same size. This will allow us to eliminate choice **C**. Choices **B** and **D** show figures that are not similar, so they can also be eliminated. This leaves **A** as our answer.

Exercise 4.2

a. $\dfrac{Rise}{Run} = \dfrac{6}{3}$, so the slope = 2.

b. $\dfrac{Rise}{Run} = \dfrac{4}{5}$, so the slope = $\dfrac{4}{5}$.

c. We can rewrite the equation as $y = \dfrac{1}{3}x - \dfrac{5}{3}$, so the slope is equal to $\dfrac{1}{3}$.

d. The slope of this line is equal to 2, so the line perpendicular to it will have a slope equal to the negative reciprocal of 2, which is $-\dfrac{1}{2}$.

e. A square can be divided into two 45-45-90 right triangles. The ratio of the sides in a 45-45-90 right triangle is always $x:x: x\sqrt{2}$, so the hypotenuse (which is the diagonal of the square) will be $5\sqrt{2}$.

f. If the diagonal of the square is $7\sqrt{2}$, this is the same as the hypotenuse of a 45-45-90 right triangle with sides of 7. So the square's sides will have a length of 7, and, therefore, an area of 49 sq. units.

g. Your drawing should look like this:

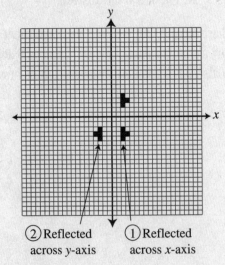

② Reflected across y-axis   ① Reflected across x-axis

h. Your drawing should look like this:

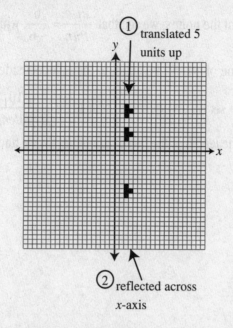

① translated 5 units up

② reflected across *x*-axis

i. First, plot these points and draw a line between them. Now draw the right triangle of which this line is the hypotenuse. This right triangle has sides 6 and 8, so its hypotenuse (which is the distance between the points) must be 10.

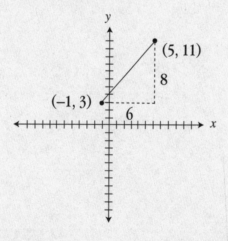

j. Here are some counterexamples: If $n = 2$, $n + 2$ (which is 4) is not prime. If $n = 7$, $n + 2$ (which is 9) is not prime.

1 B The line $x = 5$ goes straight up and down through point 5 on the *x*-axis. Only shape **B** could look the same on both sides if a vertical line were placed in the middle of the *x*-axis.

2 B This line goes up and to the left, so we know it has negative slope; this allows us to eliminate **D**. If we count the points, we see that $\dfrac{Rise}{Run} = \dfrac{6}{-6}$, which equals -1.

3 C We know that the cosine of 40 will be equal to the adjacent side (which is 10) over the hypotenuse. So we can set up an equation: $\cos(40) = \dfrac{10}{Hypotenuse}$. If we solve for the hypotenuse, which is the length of the flight path of the fly, we find that it is equal to 13.05 meters.

Exercise 5

a. *Half the value of x is equal to 6 times the difference between 24 and 12* becomes

$$\frac{1}{2}x = 6(24-12)$$

b. *78 is less than twice the product of x and 18* becomes

$$78 < 2(x \times 18)$$

c. *One-fifth of the difference between 6 and x is equal to twice the product of y and 5* becomes

$$\frac{1}{5}(6-x) = 2(y \times 5)$$

d. To begin factoring $x^2 + 3x + 10$, we find the ways we can factor 10. The number 10 can factor as 1 and 10 or 2 and 5. We can get the coefficient of 3 by subtracting 2 from 5, so we set up our parentheses:

$$(x \quad 5)\,(x \quad 2)$$

and we set our signs to add 5 and subtract 2:

$$(x + 5)\,(x - 2)$$

e. Let's start by factoring $x^2 + 15x + 50$. 50 can be written as 5 times 10, so we can factor as: $(x + 10)\,(x + 5) = 0$. This means that x could be −10 or −5.

f. This series goes up by 5 at each step, so it will be a linear function, going up in a straight line. The closest match is diagram **A**.

g. This series goes up by ever-increasing values at each step. (In fact, the difference between every two points doubles.) Its corresponding diagram should be a curve that starts shallow and then rises very sharply. The closest match is diagram **C**.

h. This series goes up by ever-decreasing values (first it goes up by 30, then by 20, then by 10). Then it goes down in the same pattern. Its corresponding diagram should rise in a gentle curve and then descend in the same curve. The closest match is diagram **D**.

i. This series goes downward, first gently (by 5, then 10 units) and then sharply (by 20 and 30 units later on). Its corresponding diagram should begin by going downward slowly and then drop off sharply. The closest match is diagram **E**.

j. This series begins by decreasing sharply (by 300, then by 100) and ends up by decreasing gradually (by 10 and 5 at the end.) Its corresponding diagram should begin by going downward sharply and then level off to a gradual descent. The closest match is diagram **B**.

k. If we plug in 0 for x and solve $3(0) - 5$, we get -5. If we plug in 5 for x and solve $3(5) - 5$, we get 10.

1 A The number of bacteria increases sharply at the beginning (by about 8,000 and then by 35,000), levels off, and then drops off sharply to finish at a point somewhat higher than where it began. Choices **C** and **D** can be eliminated right away. To decide between **A** and **B**, look carefully at the beginning and ending points. On diagram **B**, the end point is lower than the starting point, but on our chart, the first value (750) is lower than the final value (6,000). This makes **A** the best choice.

2 B Let's plug in $x = -10$ for each of these functions and see what we get.

$$A = -20 + -10 = -30$$

$$B = -30 + 100 = 70$$

$$C = -50 - 20 = -70$$

$$D = -(-10) - 10 = 0$$

Only **B** is positive, so it's our answer.

3 C The area figure goes up by ever-increasing amounts–first by 3, then by 5, then by 7. The graph should look like a curve that starts by going slowly upward and then increases more and more as it goes along. The picture that best fits this is **C**.

4 B Before you start, be sure you're clear on what the y-axis is showing you. It shows speed, so a lower position on the y-axis means that someone is moving more slowly, while a higher position means that someone is moving more quickly. We can see that at the beginning, the person speeds up to a high rate of speed, then slows down for a while, picks up more speed, and then slows down to a stop. Since the chart shows that the rider begins by picking up speed and going quickly, we can eliminate choices **A** and **D**. Choice **C** is too simple—it leaves out the center portion where the cyclist slows down and then picks up speed again. This makes **B** the best choice.

5 C We know that the phrase "twice" means we're multiplying by 2, and neither **A** nor **B** does this, so we can eliminate them. Then we see "x is 4 more than" so x must be equal to 4 plus something else. This will allow us to eliminate choice **D**, and leaves **C** as our best answer.

Exercise 6

a. The mean will be $\dfrac{60+70+95+105}{4} = 82.5$.

b. If a student has a mean of 75 on 5 tests, then we know that $\dfrac{Total\ Score}{5} = 75$. So we can solve for the total score, which must be 375.

c. If the mean of 4 numbers is 80, we know that $\dfrac{Sum\ Total}{4} = 80$, so we can solve for the sum total of these numbers, which must be 320. Two of these four numbers are 50 and 60, so if we remove their totals from 320, we get 210, which must be the sum of the other two numbers.

d. The median of the first group is 23 since 23 is the middle number. The median of the second group is 26.5, which is the average of the two middle numbers 25 and 28.

e. The mode (the number that appears the most) is 8.

f. To solve this question we can set up a proportion: $\dfrac{Blond}{Total}\ \dfrac{18}{100} = \dfrac{x}{250,000}$. If we cross-multiply and solve, we find that $x = 5,000$.

1 D Let's set up a proportion: $\dfrac{Raisins}{Mix}\ \dfrac{3}{8} = \dfrac{x}{135}$. Now if we can cross-multiply and solve, we find $x = 50.625$. This is a close approximation of choice **D**.

2 B Let's start by finding the median and mode for each of these choices. Then we can use POE to find the one we want.

> A median = 19, mode = 15
> B median = 26, mode = 26
> C median = 22, mode = 19
> D median = 19, mode = 18

Choice **B** is the only one where the mean is equal to the mode.

3 C Kim can choose from 5 kinds of ice cream and 3 toppings, so the number of different sundaes she can make is equal to 5×3, or 15.

4 B Isabel can choose from 3 salads, 5 main dishes, and 2 desserts, so the number of different meals she can choose from is equal to $3 \times 5 \times 2$, or 30.

5 B The total number of socks in the drawer is equal to 20, of which 8 are red, so her chance of drawing a red sock at random is $\frac{8}{20}$, which is equal to $\frac{2}{5}$.

6 C There is a total of 25 marbles in the bowl. What we want to draw is either a blue or green marble, of which there are $8 + 6 = 14$. So the chance of drawing either a blue or a green marble will be $\frac{14}{25}$.

7 John can choose from 5 shirts, 4 pants, and 8 pairs of socks, so the number of different outfits he could wear is equal to $5 \times 4 \times 8$, or 160.

8 B The total number of fruits sold is $8 + 25 + 13 + 8 + 6 = 60$. Of those 60 fruits, 8 oranges were sold. So the chance that the next fruit sold will be an orange is $\frac{8}{60}$, or $\frac{2}{15}$.

9a. Your drawing should look like this:

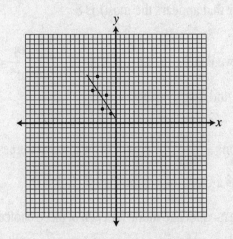

9b. The line goes down and to the right, so it has negative slope. Further, it is steeper than a line of slope −1, so it will need to be in the range of −1 to −2.

10a. We can figure out (interpolate) the approximate number of hammers sold at store A in 1994, because it must be a bit lower than 80. So it must be about 75.

10b. Store C will probably sell the greatest number of hammers in 1998. Sales in Stores A and B are approaching 70 as time goes on; their curves are both flattening out around that point, and the two stores will probably sell about 70 hammers each in 1998. However, Store C's line is steadily increasing from year to year. It should hit 70 in 1997 and then be greater than 70 in 1998.

11a. The two months that show the greatest differences are January and March, so let's look more closely at those two months. In January, John's math score was 50 and his science score was 75, for a difference of 25. In March, John's math score was 40 and his science score was 60, for a difference of 20. The greatest difference was, therefore, in the month of January.

11b. John's science scores for these months were 75, 70, 50, 85, and 60. The mean of these numbers is 68.

11c. The range of John's math scores is from a low of 40 in March to a high of 80 in April: $80 - 40 =$ a range of 40.

Part III

Practice Tests
and Explanations

Chapter 8

Practice Test 1

Values of Trigonometric Functions

Angle	Sin	Cos	Tan	Angle	Sin	Cos	Tan
1°	0.0175	0.9998	0.0175	46°	0.7193	0.6947	1.0355
2°	0.0349	0.9994	0.0349	47°	0.7314	0.6820	1.0724
3°	0.0523	0.9986	0.0524	48°	0.7431	0.6691	1.1106
4°	0.0698	0.9976	0.0699	49°	0.7547	0.6561	1.1504
5°	0.0872	0.9962	0.0875	50°	0.7660	0.6428	1.1918
6°	0.1045	0.9945	0.1051	51°	0.7771	0.6293	1.2349
7°	0.1219	0.9925	0.1227	52°	0.7880	0.6157	1.2799
8°	0.1392	0.9903	0.1405	53°	0.7986	0.6018	1.3270
9°	0.1564	0.9877	0.1584	54°	0.8090	0.5878	1.3764
10°	0.1736	0.9848	0.1763	55°	0.8192	0.5736	1.4281
11°	0.1908	0.9816	0.1944	56°	0.8290	0.5592	1.4826
12°	0.2079	0.9781	0.2126	57°	0.8387	0.5446	1.5399
13°	0.2250	0.9744	0.2309	58°	0.8480	0.5299	1.6003
14°	0.2419	0.9703	0.2493	59°	0.8572	0.5150	1.6643
15°	0.2588	0.9659	0.2679	60°	0.8660	0.5000	1.7321
16°	0.2756	0.9613	0.2867	61°	0.8746	0.4848	1.8040
17°	0.2924	0.9563	0.3057	62°	0.8829	0.4695	1.8807
18°	0.3090	0.9511	0.3249	63°	0.8910	0.4540	1.9626
19°	0.3256	0.9455	0.3443	64°	0.8988	0.4384	2.0503
20°	0.3420	0.9397	0.3640	65°	0.9063	0.4226	2.1445
21°	0.3584	0.9336	0.3839	66°	0.9135	0.4067	2.2460
22°	0.3746	0.9272	0.4040	67°	0.9205	0.3907	2.3559
23°	0.3907	0.9205	0.4245	68°	0.9272	0.3746	2.4751
24°	0.4067	0.9135	0.4452	69°	0.9336	0.3584	2.6051
25°	0.4226	0.9063	0.4663	70°	0.9397	0.3420	2.7475
26°	0.4384	0.8988	0.4877	71°	0.9455	0.3256	2.9042
27°	0.4540	0.8910	0.5095	72°	0.9511	0.3090	3.0777
28°	0.4695	0.8829	0.5317	73°	0.9563	0.2924	3.2709
29°	0.4848	0.8746	0.5543	74°	0.9613	0.2756	3.4874
30°	0.5000	0.8660	0.5774	75°	0.9659	0.2588	3.7321
31°	0.5150	0.8572	0.6009	76°	0.9703	0.2419	4.0108
32°	0.5299	0.8480	0.6249	77°	0.9744	0.2250	4.3315
33°	0.5446	0.8387	0.6494	78°	0.9781	0.2079	4.7046
34°	0.5592	0.8290	0.6745	79°	0.9816	0.1908	5.1446
35°	0.5736	0.8192	0.7002	80°	0.9848	0.1736	5.6713
36°	0.5878	0.8090	0.7265	81°	0.9877	0.1564	6.3138
37°	0.6018	0.7986	0.7536	82°	0.9903	0.1392	7.1154
38°	0.6157	0.7880	0.7813	83°	0.9925	0.1219	8.1443
39°	0.6293	0.7771	0.8098	84°	0.9945	0.1045	9.5144
40°	0.6428	0.7660	0.8391	85°	0.9962	0.0872	11.4301
41°	0.6561	0.7547	0.8693	86°	0.9976	0.0698	14.3007
42°	0.6691	0.7431	0.9004	87°	0.9986	0.0523	19.0811
43°	0.6820	0.7314	0.9325	88°	0.9994	0.0349	28.6363
44°	0.6947	0.7193	0.9657	89°	0.9998	0.0175	57.2900
45°	0.7071	0.7071	1.0000	90°	1.0000	0.0000	------

Formula Sheet

Volume Formulas

cube............$V = e^3$

cylinder.........$V = \pi r^2 h$

cone...........$V = \dfrac{1}{3}\pi r^2 h$

regular prism.....$V = Bh$ (B = area of the base)

sphere..........$V = \dfrac{4}{3}\pi r^3$

Area Formulas

triangle.........$A = \dfrac{1}{2}bh$

rectangle.........$A = bh$

square...........$A = s^2$

triangle.........$A = \dfrac{1}{2}h(b_1 + b_2)$

Circle Formulas

$C = 2\pi r$

$A = \pi r^2$

Surface Area Formulas

sphere..........$SA = 4\pi r^2$

cube...........$SA = 6e^2$

cylinder.........$SA = 2\pi r^2 + 2\pi rh$

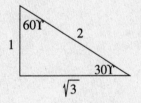

Final tips on the practice tests:

Give yourself no more than 45 minutes to complete each session. Either set an alarm or have a parent or a friend tell you when your time is up.

You are not allowed to use your calculator for the first session.

Remember that although the actual Grade 10 MCAS Math test has 42 scored questions, you will see about seven additional questions throughout the exam. These questions are called field-test (or matrix) items, and they're being tested for future exams. They won't count toward your score, but since you won't know which questions are the matrix items, you'll have to answer every question as if it counts.

Session 1, Multiple-choice Questions

(No calculator allowed)

1 Which of the following fractions is between $\frac{4}{20}$ and $\frac{7}{20}$?

A. $\frac{4}{10}$

B. $\frac{4}{40}$

C. $\frac{9}{30}$

D. $\frac{2}{5}$

	Strain 1	Strain 2	Strain 3	Strain 4
Start	5	5	5	5
Day 1	55	10	10	25
Day 2	105	15	20	45
Day 3	155	20	40	65

2 Which of the four bacteria strains will have the largest population after 8 days?

A. Strain 1

B. Strain 2

C. Strain 3

D. Strain 4

3   $(x + y)(x + z)$ is the same as:

A. $2x + x(y + z) + yz$

B. $x^2 + x(y + z) + yz$

C. $x^2 + yz + xz$

D. $x(x + y + z)$

4   Which of the following pairs of points defines a line with a slope of $\frac{1}{2}$?

A. $(0, 1)$ and $(3, 4)$

B. $(1, -1)$ and $(3, 3)$

C. $(4, 4)$ and $(6, 3)$

D. $(-2, 0)$ and $(2, 2)$

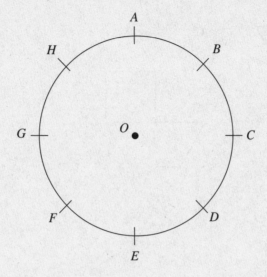

5   Point *O* is the center of the circle. Triangle *AOB* shows one example of a triangle that can be drawn by connecting *O* with two points on the edge of the circle. Which of the following triangles has the greatest perimeter?

    A. *BOD*

    B. *BOE*

    C. *EOG*

    D. *EOF*

6   If $x^2 < x$, which of the following is true?

    A. $0 > x > -1$

    B. $1 > x > 0$

    C. $x < -1$

    D. $x > 1$

7   Which of the following forms could be folded to make a pyramid?

A.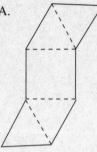

C.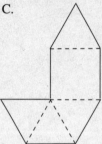

B.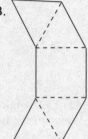

D.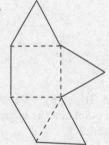

8   Angie is creating a gift bag for her party guests. The following chart shows the items she can choose from.

Candy Bars: Chocalot, Vanillarama
Hats: Blue, Red, Green
Fruit: Apple, Orange, Banana
Toys: Ball, Noisemaker

If Angie puts 1 candy bar, 1 hat, 1 piece of fruit, and 1 toy in each bag, how many different gift bags could she create?

A. 8

B. 16

C. 18

D. 36

9 $\left(\sqrt{612^2}\right)^0 + 5 =$

    A. 0

    B. 1

    C. 5

    D. 6

10 For a long-distance phone call, the phone company charges 50 cents for the first minute and 10 cents for each additional minute. If m stands for the number of minutes in a call, which of the following shows the cost of a call?

    A. $50m + 10$

    B. $10m + 50$

    C. $9m + 50$

    D. $10(m - 1) + 50$

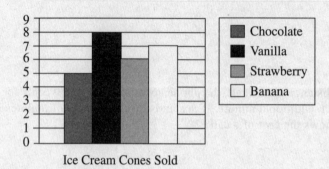

Ice Cream Cones Sold

11   This chart shows the average number of ice cream cones sold at a store on a given day. What is the probability that the next cone sold will be chocolate?

12   A statement is made that every line of symmetry for a regular hexagon will bisect one of the angles of the hexagon. Draw a sketch that shows that this statement is not always true.

Session 1, Open-response Question

13 Between 1990 and 1994, the population of Lincolnville increased from 126,000 to 152,000.

    a. What was the percent increase in the population of Lincolnville between 1990 and 1994? Round your answer to the nearest whole percent.

    b. If the population of Emmondsville was 85,000 in 1990, and its population increased by the same percentage increase as the population of Lincolnville, what would its population be in 1995? Explain your answer.

    c. If the population of Lincolnville increased by another 26,000 people from 1994 to 1998, did its rate of growth increase or decrease? Explain your answer.

Session 1, Short-answer Questions

14   The formula $p = \dfrac{a^2}{b}$ is used to calculate the value of p. If the value of a doubles and the value of b is halved, then p will increase by what factor?

15   The mean of 32, 34, x, and y is 20. What is the mean of x and y?

Use the diagram below to answer question 16.

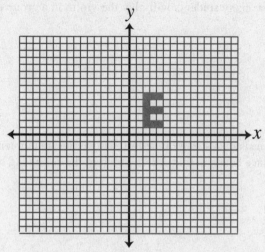

16 a. Transform the shaded *E* in the first quadrant according to the following steps:

Step 1: Reflect the *E* across the *y*-axis.

Step 2: Reflect the *E* across the *x*-axis.

Step 3: Translate the result of step II 7 units down.

Step 4: Reflect the *E* across the *y*-axis

Draw and label each of these four steps on the grid below.

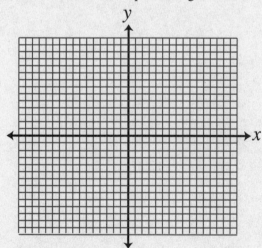

b. Describe a transformation with fewer than four steps that would achieve the same result as the transformation described in part a.

17 In a group of 240 students, 17 play the violin. If this sample is representative of all students, approximately how many students will play the violin in a group of 3,000 students?

A. 15

B. 175

C. 210

D. 220

18 David is placing beads on a string in the following order: red, green, blue, red, green, blue . . . . If he continues to place beads in this order, which of the following beads will be green?

A. the 71st bead

B. the 78th bead

C. the 81st bead

D. the 84th bead

19 On Ms. McLeary's final math test, two students scored 95, two students scored 92, three students scored 85, and one student scored 89. What was the median score for the class?

A. 89

B. 90.5

C. 91.5

D. 92

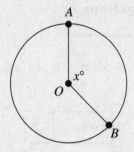

20 The circumference of circle O is 24. If minor arc AB is 8, what is the value of x?

  A. 36

  B. 60

  C. 120

  D. 150

The table below shows the number of cars sold at a certain dealership in the first six months of 1999.

January	2
February	8
March	6
April	14
May	13
June	16

21 a. On the grid below, plot the data using the months of the year as the *x*-axis.

   b. Draw a single straight line that best represents the data.

   c. Explain why you drew your line as you did.

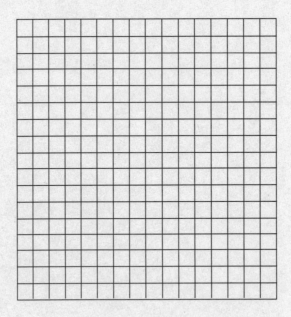

22　During a special sale, the price of a television is reduced by 10% the first day of the sale and then by an additional 4% for each successive day of the sale.

a.　If the sale price of the television after 2 days is $80, what was the original price of the television? Show how you found your answer.

b.　After 4 days, the new price of a television will be what percent of the original price of the television? Round your answer to the nearest percent, and show how you found your answer.

c.　If the original price of a television was $180, after how many days will the price of the television be less than $150?

23   Which of the lines below is perpendicular to the line $4x - y = 6$?

   A. $y = 1$

   B. $y = 0$

   C. $y = 2x + 3$

   D. $y = 8 - \left(\dfrac{1}{4}\right)x$

24   In the formula $x = \dfrac{1}{y^2}$, if the value of y is doubled, the value of x becomes:

   A.   twice as large

   B.   four times as large

   C. $\dfrac{1}{2}$ as large

   D. $\dfrac{1}{4}$ as large

Side	Area
1	1
2	4
3	9
4	16

25 Which graph best represents the relationship between the side of a square and its area?

A.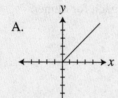

C.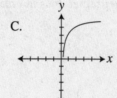

B.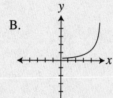

D.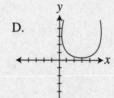

26 In a group of 117 people, 67 have brown eyes, 25 have blue eyes, 14 have green eyes, and 11 have hazel eyes. If one person is chosen at random from this group, what is the probability that the person chosen will have either brown or green eyes?

A. $\dfrac{2}{3}$

B. $\dfrac{9}{13}$

C. $\dfrac{95}{117}$

D. $\dfrac{11}{12}$

27 If the width of a rectangle is 10 inches greater than its length, and the perimeter of the rectangle is 180 inches, then what is the area of the rectangle?

A. 1,000 square inches

B. 1,200 square inches

C. 1,600 square inches

D. 2,000 square inches

28 Kim's father says, "If you like spinach, then I will make some for dinner." Which of the following would show that Kim's father did not follow through with his statement?

A. Kim likes spinach and her father makes spinach for dinner.

B. Kim likes spinach and her father does not make spinach for dinner.

C. Kim does not like spinach and her father makes spinach for dinner.

D. Kim does not like spinach and her father does not make spinach for dinner.

A.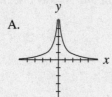

C.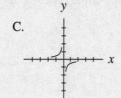

B.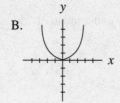

D.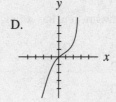

29 Which of these graphs shows a function that is symmetrical across the line $x = y$?

   A. Figure A

   B. Figure B

   C. Figure C

   D. Figure D

30 If two sides of triangle are 4 and 8, which of the following is not a possible perimeter of the triangle?

   A. 16

   B. 18

   C. 21

   D. 23

31 A rectangular swimming pool with dimensions 2 feet by 3 feet by 4 feet is being filled by a hose that produces 6 cubic feet of water per minute. At this rate, how many minutes will it take to fill the pool?

A. 6

B. 4

C. 3

D. 2

32 Which of the following sets has a range of 50 and a mean of 25?

A. 10, 20, 40, 60

B. 10, 13, 17, 60

C. 10, 11, 19, 40

D. 10, 16, 24, 50

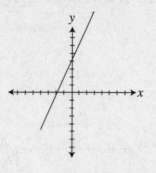

33 Which of the following equations could describe the line on the graph above?

A. $y = \dfrac{1}{3}x + 10$

B. $y = 3x + 10$

C. $y = -3x + 10$

D. $y = 3x - 10$

34 Which of the following statements is always true?

A. The sum of two rational numbers is always greater than either of the numbers.

B. The product of two rational numbers is always greater than either of the numbers.

C. The sum of two rational numbers is always rational.

D. The square root of a rational number is always rational.

35   Which of the following functions will have the largest value for $x = 10$?

A. $f(x) = x^2 + 2x$

B. $f(x) = 12x + 5$

C. $f(x) = 1^x$

D. $f(x) = x^3 - x^2$

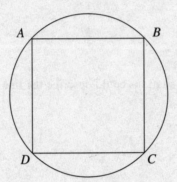

36   If square $ABCD$ is inscribed in a circle with area 9π, what is the area of $ABCD$?

A.   18

B. $18\sqrt{2}$

C.   36

D. $36\sqrt{2}$

37 If $3 \geq x \geq -4$, which of the following gives the range of possible values of x^2?

    A. $-16 \leq x^2 \leq 9$

    B. $-9 \leq x^2 \leq 16$

    C. $0 \leq x^2 \leq 16$

    D. $9 \leq x^2 \leq 16$

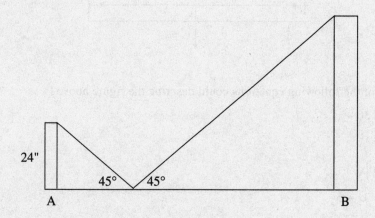

38 Michelle wants to measure the size of building B. By placing herself $\frac{1}{5}$ of the way from building A to building B, she can see the tops of both buildings at an angle of ascent of 45 degrees. She knows that building A is 24 feet tall. How tall is building B?

    A. 48 feet

    B. 69 feet

    C. 96 feet

    D. 120 feet

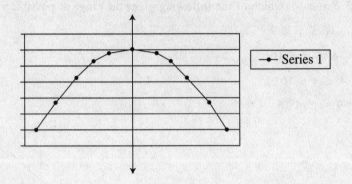

39 Which of the following equations could describe the figure above?

A. $y = 30 - x^2$

B. $y = x^2$

C. $y = |x|$

D. $y = 3x + 5$

40 Harris throws a ball down to the ground from a building with a height of 80 feet. If the ball travels in a straight line and lands at a point 60 feet away from the base of the building, how far does the ball travel?

A. 70 feet

B. 80 feet

C. 90 feet

D. 100 feet

Session 3, Open-response Questions

41 A sum of money is deposited in a bank account, where it earns 10% interest per year. No other deposits or withdrawals are made. After 3 years, the account holds $798.60.

    a. How much was in the bank account originally? Show your work.

    b. After how many years will the amount of money in the account be more than $1,000? Show your work.

    c. Write a mathematical expression to show how much money will be in the account after any given number of years.

42 A Worcester auto dealership pays $34,000 in rent and other general expenses every month. Furthermore, this dealership buys their cars for $15,550 and sells them for $16,400. The owner of the dealership, Gil, thinks that he needs to sell 50 cars every month to break even.

    a. Is Gil correct in his estimation that he needs to sell 50 cars per month to break even? If he was wrong, what was the right answer? Show how you found your result.

    b. If the rent of the auto dealership went up $2,720 per month, how many cars would Gil need to sell to make a profit in a month? Explain how you found your answer.

    c. Gil decides that he needs to create a formula to help him figure out his monthly losses or profits. Write a formula to help Gil determine his monthly losses or profits, using the variables listed below.

- Rent and other expenses: R
- Buying cost for the dealership to buy each car: B
- Selling price for each car: S
- Number of cars sold in a month: N
- Profit or loss per month: P

Chapter 9

Practice Test 1
Answers and Explanations

Session 1. Multiple-choice Questions

Multiple-choice answers
Session 1:

1	C
2	C
3	B
4	D
5	B
6	B
7	A
8	D
9	D
10	D

Session 2:

17	C
18	A
19	B
20	C

1 Which of the following fractions is between $\frac{4}{20}$ and $\frac{7}{20}$?

A. $\frac{4}{10}$

B. $\frac{4}{40}$

C. $\frac{9}{30}$

D. $\frac{2}{5}$

1 C The easiest way to solve this problem is to convert each of the answer choices to a fraction with a denominator of 20. If we multiply the top and bottom of choice **A** by 2, the fraction becomes $\frac{8}{20}$, which is too big. If we divide the top and bottom of **B** by 2, we get $\frac{2}{20}$, which is too small. If we multiply the top and bottom of **C** by $\frac{2}{3}$, we get $\frac{6}{20}$, which is between $\frac{4}{20}$ and $\frac{7}{20}$.

	Strain 1	Strain 2	Strain 3	Strain 4
Start	5	5	5	5
Day 1	55	10	10	25
Day 2	105	15	20	45
Day 3	155	20	40	65

2 Which of the four bacteria strains will have the largest population after 8 days?

A. Strain 1

B. Strain 2

C. Strain 3

D. Strain 4

2 C Looking at Strain 1, the pattern goes 5 (+50) 55 (+50) 105 . . . so Strain 1 increases by 50 each day. Likewise, Strain 2 increases by 5 each day, and Strain 4 increases by 20 each day. Of these three strains, Strain 1 will increase the most and have a population of 405 after 8 days. However, the pattern for Strain 3 goes 5 (×2) 10 (×2) 20 (×2) 40 . . . so Strain 3 doubles each day. This will increase much faster and have a population of 1,280 after 8 days. That's **C**.

Session 3:

23	D
24	D
25	B
26	B
27	D
28	B
29	C
30	A
31	B
32	B
33	B
34	C
35	D
36	A
37	C
38	C
39	A
40	D

3    $(x + y) (x + z)$ is the same as:

A. $2x + x(y + z) + yz$

B. $x^2 + x(y + z) + yz$

C. $x^2 + yz + xz$

D. $x(x + y + z)$

3   B   If we multiply $(x + y) (x + z)$ out, we get $x^2 + xz + xy + yz$. Likewise, if we multiply out choice **B**, we get $x^2 + xz + xy + yz$. You could also Plug In for all the variables here. Say $x = 3$, $y = 4$, and $z = 5$. Then it's $(3 + 4)$ $(3 + 5)$, which is $(7) (8)$, or 56. Then, just plug those numbers into all the answer choices until you get 56. Check out **B**: $x^2 + x(y + z) + yz$ becomes $9 + 3(4+5) + 20$, which is $9 + 27 + 20$, or 56. Bingo!

4   Which of the following pairs of points defines a line with a slope of $\frac{1}{2}$?

A. (0, 1) and (3, 4)

B. (1, –1) and (3, 3)

C. (4, 4) and (6, 3)

D. (–2, 0) and (2, 2)

4   D   To find the slope, just find the $\frac{rise}{run}$. Choice **A** has a slope of $\frac{3}{3}$, or 1. Choice **B** has a slope of $\frac{4}{2}$, or 2. Choice **C** has a slope of $-\frac{1}{2}$, and choice **D** has a slope of $\frac{2}{4}$, which is the same as $\frac{1}{2}$.

5   Point *O* is the center of the circle. Triangle *AOB* shows one example of a triangle that can be drawn by connecting *O* with two points on the edge of the circle. Which of the following triangles has the greatest perimeter?

A. *BOD*

B. *BOE*

C. *EOG*

D. EOF

5   B   Since all of the radii in a circle are equal, every triangle made between *O* and any points on the edge of the circle will have two sides that are equal; they will only differ in the length of their third side. The triangle that has the largest third side will have the largest perimeter. We also know that a larger side of a triangle will always be opposite a larger angle, so the triangle that has the largest angle at the center will have the largest perimeter. Of the choices listed, triangle *BOE* has the largest angle at point *O*, so it will also have the largest perimeter.

6   If $x^2 < x$, which of the following is true?

   A. $0 > x > -1$

   B. $1 > x > 0$

   C. $x < -1$

   D. $x > 1$

6   B Plug in some numbers, but remember that when you square a number, it always gets bigger, except for fractions between 0 and 1. For instance, $\dfrac{1}{2}^{2} = \dfrac{1}{4}$. So if $x = \dfrac{1}{2}$, then $x^2 < x$.

7   Which of the following forms could be folded to make a pyramid?

A.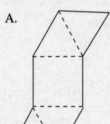

C.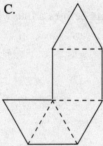

B.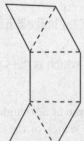

D.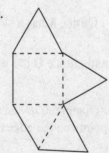

7   A On figures **B**, **C** and **D**, faces 1 and 4 will overlap on one side of the figure, leaving a missing face on the other side. So **A** is the correct choice.

8   Angie is creating a gift bag for her party guests. The following chart shows the items she can choose from.

Candy Bars: Chocalot, Vanillarama
Hats: Blue, Red, Green
Fruit: Apple, Orange, Banana
Toys: Ball, Noisemaker

If Angie puts 1 candy bar, 1 hat, 1 piece of fruit, and 1 toy in each bag, how many different gift bags could she create?

A. 8

B. 16

C. 18

D. 36

8   D   The number of different combinations will be equal to the product of the items she can choose from. She can choose from 2 candy bars, 3 hats, 3 fruits, and 2 toys, so the number of combinations will be equal to $2 \times 3 \times 3 \times 2$, or 36.

9    $\left(\sqrt{612^2} \right)^0 + 5 =$

A. 0

B. 1

C. 5

D. 6

9   D   The test writers can't be asking you to calculate such a complicated number, so they must be looking for a mathematical rule. Since anything to the 0 power is equal to 1, the problem actually becomes $1 + 5$, or 6.

10   For a long-distance phone call, the phone company charges 50 cents for the first minute and 10 cents for each additional minute. If m stands for the number of minutes in a call, which of the following shows the cost of a call?

A. $50m + 10$

B. $10m + 50$

C. $9m + 50$

D. $10(m - 1) + 50$

10 D   Plug in a number to make the math easier. Let's suppose our call is 5 minutes long. So in this case our $m = 5$. The phone company will charge us 50 cents for the first minute and then 10 cents for the 4 remaining minutes. We can write this as $50 + 10 \times 4$, or 90. Which choice says this? **D** does.

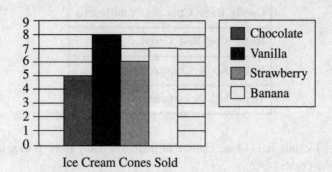

Ice Cream Cones Sold

11 This chart shows the average number of ice cream cones sold at a store on a given day. What is the probability that the next cone sold will be chocolate?

11 $\dfrac{5}{26}$ Since there were 5 + 8 + 6 + 7 = 26 total cones sold, of which 5 were chocolate, the probability that the next one will be chocolate is $\dfrac{5}{26}$.

12 A statement is made that every line of symmetry for a regular hexagon will bisect one of the angles of the hexagon. Draw a sketch that shows that this statement is not always true.

12   Here is one way you could draw the figure as a counterexample:

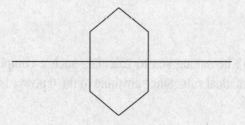

Session 1. Open-response Questions

13 Between 1990 and 1994, the population of Lincolnville increased from 126,000 to 152,000.

    a. What was the percent increase in the population of Lincolnville between 1990 and 1994? Round your answer to the nearest whole percent.

13a.   **21%** Percent increase is always $\dfrac{Difference}{Original}$. The difference in population amounts to 26,000 people, so the percent increase is equal to $\dfrac{26,000}{126,000}$ or about 21%.

    b. If the population of Emmondsville was 85,000 in 1990, and its population increased by the same percentage increase as the population of Lincolnville, what would its population be in 1995? Explain your answer.

13b.   **102,850** Let's start by taking 21% of 85,000: $\dfrac{21}{100} \times 85,000 = 17,850$. So if the population of 85,000 increases by 21%, it will increase by 17,850, which raises it to a total of 102,850.

    c. If the population of Lincolnville increased by another 26,000 people from 1994 to 1998, did its rate of growth increase or decrease? Explain your answer.

13c.   **Its rate of growth decreases.** If it increases by another 26,000 people, the percent change will be $\dfrac{26,000}{152,000}$, which comes to 17% growth.

14 The formula $p = \dfrac{a^2}{b}$ is used to calculate the value of p. If the value of a doubles and the value of b is halved, then p will increase by what factor?

14 8 Let's plug in some numbers. If $a = 2$ and $b = 4$, then p will be equal to $\dfrac{2^2}{4}$, or 1. If a doubles, it is now equal to 4. If b is halved, it is now equal to 2. So p will be equal to $\dfrac{4^2}{2}$, or 8. The value of p has gone from 1 to 8, so it has increased by a factor of 8.

15 The mean of 32, 34, x, and y is 20. What is the mean of x and y?

15 7 If the mean of any four numbers is 20, then we know that their sum total must be equal to 80. This means that $32 + 34 + x + y = 80$. We can then subtract 32 and 34 from each side of the equation to determine that $x + y = 14$. So their average is 7.

Session 1, Open-response Question

Use the diagram below to answer question 16.

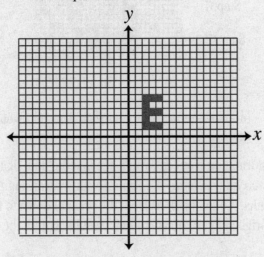

16 a. Transform the shaded *E* in the first quadrant according to the following steps:

Step 1: Reflect the *E* across the *y*-axis.

Step 2: Reflect the *E* across the *x*-axis.

Step 3: Translate the result of step II 7 units down.

Step 4: Reflect the *E* across the *y*-axis

Draw and label each of these four steps on the grid below.

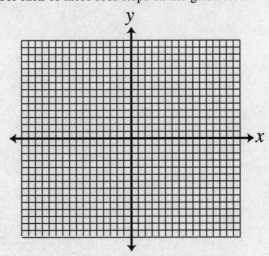

16a.

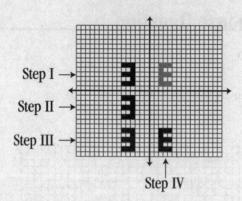

Step I →
Step II →
Step III →

Step IV

    b.   Describe a transformation with fewer than four steps that would achieve the same result as the transformation described in part a.

16b.   If you did your transformation correctly, you'll see that the final figure ends up directly below the original figure, so we could achieve the same result by translating the original figure down a certain number of units. Count the units from the original down to the final figure, and you'll see that translating the original figure down 14 units would achieve the same result.

17 In a group of 240 students, 17 play the violin. If this sample is representative of all students, approximately how many students will play the violin in a group of 3,000 students?

   A. 15

   B. 175

   C. 210

   D. 220

17 C To solve this, we should set up a proportion: $\dfrac{240}{17} = \dfrac{3,000}{x}$. If we cross-multiply, we get $x = 212.5$. This is approximately 210.

18 David is placing beads on a string in the following order: red, green, blue, red, green, blue . . . . If he continues to place beads in this order, which of the following beads will be green?

   A. the 71st bead

   B. the 78th bead

   C. the 81st bead

   D. the 84th bead

18 A One way to solve this pattern problem is to write out the pattern. A green bead will appear in places 2, 5, 8, 11, 14, 17, 20 . . . write out as many steps as you need to until you see the pattern. A green bead appears every 3 beads after bead number 2, so we know that a green bead will also be at bead 32, 62, and 92. From 62 we know that a green will also be beads 65, 68, and 71.

19 On Ms. McLeary's final math test, two students scored 95, two students scored 92, three students scored 85, and one student scored 89. What was the median score for the class?

   A. 89

   B. 90.5

   C. 91.5

   D. 92

19 B To find the median, first arrange the scores in numerical order: 85, 85, 85, 89, 92, 92, 95, 95. Since there are an even number of values, we need to average the two middle numbers: 89 and 92. Their average is 90.5.

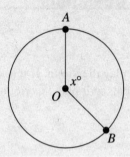

20 The circumference of circle O is 24. If minor arc AB is 8, what is the value of x?

A. 36

B. 60

C. 120

D. 150

20 C Since the arc AB is 8, and the circumference is 24, then the arc AB is $\frac{1}{3}$ of the circumference of the circle. This means that angle x will be $\frac{1}{3}$ of the 360 degrees in a circle, or 120 degrees.

Session 2. Open-response Questions

The table below shows the number of cars sold at a certain dealership in the first six months of 1999.

January	2
February	8
March	6
April	14
May	13
June	16

21 a.   On the grid below, plot the data using the months of the year as the *x*-axis.

b.   Draw a single straight line that best represents the data.

c.   Explain why you drew your line as you did.

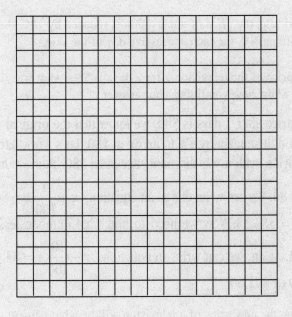

21a. and b.

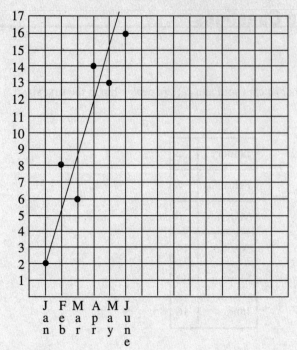

21c. This line best fits the data because it goes through the middle of the set of points, and so approximates their mean.

22 During a special sale, the price of a television is reduced by 10% the first day of the sale and then by an additional 4% for each successive day of the sale.

a. If the sale price of the television after 2 days is $80, what was the original price of the television? Show how you found your answer.

22a. $92.60. If the price after 2 days is $80, we know that the original price has been reduced by 10% and then again by 4% to arrive at $80. Let's work backwards one step at a time. What price, with a 4% discount, becomes $80? Some value minus 4% of itself must equal $80. We can write this as an equation: $x - \dfrac{4}{100}x = 80$. If we solve for x, we find that $x = \$83.33$. Now we need to find what number, less 10% of itself, is equal to $83.33. Again, we can write an equation: $y - \dfrac{10}{100}y = 83.33$. Solve for y, and we get $92.59 or $92.60.

b. After 4 days, the new price of a television will be what percent of the original price of the television? Round your answer to the nearest percent, and show how you found your answer.

22b. **83%.** Let's assume that a television starts at $100. After 1 day, it will decrease in price by 10% to $90. The next day it will reduce by 4%. 4% of $90 is equal to $\dfrac{4}{100} \times 90$, which is approximately $3.60, so the price will drop to $86.40. On the third day it will drop another 4% to $82.94. On the fourth day it will drop another 4% to $83.08. This final number is about 83% of the original price.

   c. If the original price of a television was $180, after how many days will the price of the television be less than $150?

22c. **6 days.** If a television starts at $800 on the first day it will drop 10% to $172. On the second day it will drop 4% of $172, which is $28.80, to $691.20. On the third day it will drop 4% of that, which is equal to $27.65, to $663.55. At this point, you can probably see that it will drop approximately $25 per day. So on the sixth day, the price will drop below $600

23 Which of the lines below is perpendicular to the line $4x - y = 6$?

A. $y = 1$

B. $y = 0$

C. $y = 2x + 3$

D. $y = 8 - \left(\dfrac{1}{4}\right)x$

23 D If we rewrite the equation $4x - y = 6$ in standard slope-intercept form, it becomes $y = 4x - 6$. This tells us that the slope of the line is 4. Remember that a line perpendicular to a line of slope m will have a slope equal to the negative reciprocal of m. So the line perpendicular to the line $y = 4x - 6$ must have a slope of $-\dfrac{1}{4}$. Only choice **D** has this slope.

24 In the formula $x = \dfrac{1}{y^2}$, if the value of y is doubled, the value of x becomes:

A. twice as large

B. four times as large

C. $\dfrac{1}{2}$ as large

D. $\dfrac{1}{4}$ as large

Side	Area
1	1
2	4
3	9
4	16

24 D Let's try plugging in a value for y. If y is 2, then x is $\dfrac{1}{4}$. If y doubles to 4, then x becomes $\dfrac{1}{16}$. So the value of x is reduced by one-fourth.

25 Which graph best represents the relationship between the side of a square and its area?

A.
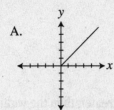

C.
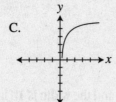

B.
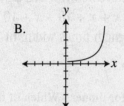

D.
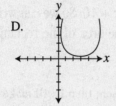

25 B Use POE. Since these numbers differ by greater and greater values as the numbers get bigger, choices **A**, **C**, and **D** can be eliminated.

26 In a group of 117 people, 67 have brown eyes, 25 have blue eyes, 14 have green eyes, and 11 have hazel eyes. If one person is chosen at random from this group, what is the probability that the person chosen will have either brown or green eyes?

A. $\dfrac{2}{3}$

B. $\dfrac{9}{13}$

C. $\dfrac{95}{117}$

D. $\dfrac{11}{12}$

26 B The total number of people in the group is 117. The number of people who have the quality we want (brown or green eyes) is equal to 67 + 14, or 81. So, the probability that the person chosen will have brown or green eyes is $\dfrac{81}{117}$, which reduces to $\dfrac{9}{13}$.

27 If the width of a rectangle is 10 inches greater than its length, and the perimeter of the rectangle is 180 inches, then what is the area of the rectangle?

    A. 1,000 square inches

    B. 1,200 square inches

    C. 1,600 square inches

    D. 2,000 square inches

27 D If we call the length of the rectangle x, and the width is 10 inches greater, then the width is $10 + x$. The perimeter of the rectangle, which is 180 sq. inches, can therefore be written as the sum of the 4 sides, which are x, x, $x + 10$, and $x + 10$. So we can write $x + x + x + 10 + x + 10 = 180$ sq. inches, and see that $x = 40$. Then the area of the rectangle is length times width, or 50×40, which is 2,000 sq. inches.

28 Kim's father says, "If you like spinach, then I will make some for dinner." Which of the following would show that Kim's father did not follow through with his statement?

    A. Kim likes spinach and her father makes spinach for dinner.

    B. Kim likes spinach and her father does not make spinach for dinner.

    C. Kim does not like spinach and her father makes spinach for dinner.

    D. Kim does not like spinach and her father does not make spinach for dinner.

28 B Remember that an if-then statement is shown to be false when the IF part is true, but the THEN part is false. So we're looking for a statement that says that Kim likes spinach, but her father does not make it for dinner. That's **B**.

A.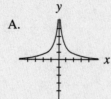

C.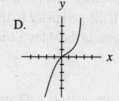

B.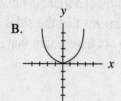

D.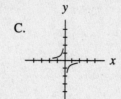

29 Which of these graphs shows a function that is symmetrical across the line $x = y$?

A. Figure A

B. Figure B

C. Figure C

D. Figure D

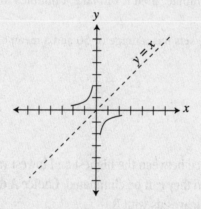

29 C The line $x = y$ goes up at a 45-degree angle through the origin. If you draw this line, the only figure that is symmetrical on each side of it is choice **C**.

30 If two sides of triangle are 4 and 8, which of the following is not a possible perimeter of the triangle?

A. 16

B. 18

C. 21

D. 23

30 A Remember the rule that the sum of every two sides of a triangle must be larger than the third side. Let's try choice **A**. If the perimeter is 16, this means that the sides are 4, 8, and 4. This is not a possible triangle because the sides 4 and 4 do not have a sum that is larger than 8. So this is our answer.

31 A rectangular swimming pool with dimensions 2 feet by 3 feet by 4 feet is being filled by a hose that produces 6 cubic feet of water per minute. At this rate, how many minutes will it take to fill the pool?

A. 6

B. 4

C. 3

D. 2

31 B First, let's find the volume of the pool. The volume is $2 \times 3 \times 4$, or 24 cubic feet. If 6 cubic feet flow into the pool every minute, then it will take 4 minutes for the pool to fill.

32 Which of the following sets has a range of 50 and a mean of 25?

A. 10, 20, 40, 60

B. 10, 13, 17, 60

C. 10, 11, 19, 40

D. 10, 16, 24, 50

32 B The range is the difference between the highest and lowest values. Use POE: Choices **C** and **D** do not have a range of 50, so they can be eliminated. Choice **A** does not have a mean of 25, so it can also be eliminated. That leaves us with **B**.

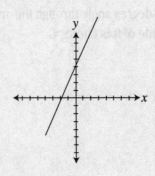

33 Which of the following equations could describe the line on the graph above?

A. $y = \frac{1}{3}x + 10$

B. $y = 3x + 10$

C. $y = -3x + 10$

D. $y = 3x - 10$

33 B Use POE! Since the line crosses the y-axis in the region where the values of y are positive, we can eliminate choice **D**, which has a negative y-intercept. Since the slope of the line is positive, we can eliminate **C**. Finally, the slope of the line is steeper than a line with slope 1, so we can eliminate choice **A**.

34 Which of the following statements is always true?

A. The sum of two rational numbers is always greater than either of the numbers.

B. The product of two rational numbers is always greater than either of the numbers.

C. The sum of two rational numbers is always rational.

D. The square root of a rational number is always rational.

34 C Use POE! We can find counterexamples for choices **A**, **B**, and **D**. Choice **A** is not always true because negative numbers can be rational: $-5 + -3$ is not bigger than either one of these numbers. Choice **B** is not always true because $0 \times 5 = 0$. Choice **D** is not always true because the square root of 10 is not rational.

35 Which of the following functions will have the largest value for $x = 10$?

A. $f(x) = x^2 + 2x$

B. $f(x) = 12x + 5$

C. $f(x) = 1^x$

D. $f(x) = x^3 - x^2$

35 D If we plug in 10 for x in the functions, **A** becomes 120, **B** becomes 125, **C** becomes 1, and **D** becomes 900. 900 is definitely the largest.

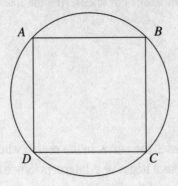

36 If square *ABCD* is inscribed in a circle with area 9π, what is the area of *ABCD*?

    A. 18

    B. $18\sqrt{2}$

    C. 36

    D. $36\sqrt{2}$

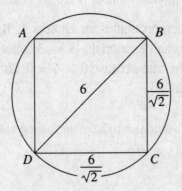

36 A Since the area of the circle is 9π, we know that its radius must be 3 and its diameter must be 6. The diameter of the circle is also the diagonal of the square. Knowing that the diagonal is 6, we can solve for the sides because the diagonal is the hypotenuse of the 45:45:90 right triangles that can be drawn inside the square. Since the hypotenuse of a 45:45:90 triangle is always a factor of $\sqrt{2}$ times either of the legs, we know that each side of the square measures $\dfrac{6}{\sqrt{2}}$. The area of the square is therefore $\dfrac{6}{\sqrt{2}} \times \dfrac{6}{\sqrt{2}}$, or 18 sq. units.

37 If $3 \geq x \geq -4$, which of the following gives the range of possible values of x^2?

    A. $-16 \leq x^2 \leq 9$

    B. $-9 \leq x^2 \leq 16$

    C. $0 \leq x^2 \leq 16$

    D. $9 \leq x^2 \leq 16$

37 C This problem is a bit sneaky. Even though x can be negative, x^2 cannot. So choices **A** and **B** can be eliminated. Since x could be 0, so could x^2. This will allow us to eliminate choice **D**, so the answer must be **C**.

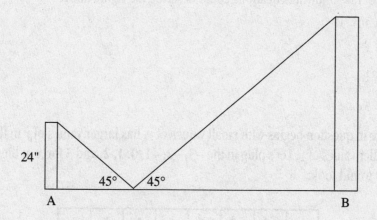

38 Michelle wants to measure the size of building B. By placing herself $\frac{1}{5}$ of the way from building A to building B, she can see the tops of both buildings at an angle of ascent of 45 degrees. She knows that building A is 24 feet tall. How tall is building B?

    A. 48 feet

    B. 69 feet

    C. 96 feet

    D. 120 feet

38 C The two triangles are similar since they each have a 90-degree angle and a 45-degree angle in them. Therefore, their sides are proportional to each other. Since Michelle stands $\frac{1}{5}$ of the way from building A to building B, we know that she is 4 times as far from building B as she is from building A. Each side of the larger triangle is therefore 4 times the size of the corresponding side of the smaller triangle. The height of building B must be 24×4, or 96 feet.

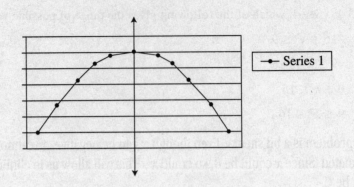

Series 1

39 Which of the following equations could describe the figure above?

A. $y = 30 - x^2$

B. $y = x^2$

C. $y = |x|$

D. $y = 3x + 5$

39 A The figure in question begins with small values of y, has larger values of y in the middle, and ends with smaller values of y. Let's plug in the $-3, -2, -1, 0, 1, 2,$ and 3 for x in these functions and see how they would look:

x	-3	-2	-1	0	1	2	3
A	21	24	29	30	29	24	21
B	9	4	1	0	1	4	9
C	3	2	1	0	1	2	3
D	-4	-1	2	5	8	11	14

Now use POE. As you can see, functions **B** and **C** are larger at the beginning and end, and smaller in the middle; they can be eliminated. We can also eliminate choice **D** since it keeps growing.

40 Harris throws a ball down to the ground from a building with a height of 80 feet. If the ball travels in a straight line and lands at a point 60 feet away from the base of the building, how far does the ball travel?

A. 70 feet

B. 80 feet

C. 90 feet

D. 100 feet

CRACKING THE MCAS GRADE 10 MATHEMATICS

40 D You probably noticed that the flight of the ball goes along the hypotenuse of the right triangle with sides 60 and 80. Before we use the Pythagorean theorem, start by Ballparking! We know that the hypotenuse is bigger than the side of 80, so we can eliminate choices **A** and **B**. If you can't get any further, we at least can take a good guess. Now let's use the Pythagorean theorem. We know that $a^2 + b^2 = c^2$, so $60^2 + 80^2 = c^2$. If we calculate this out, we get $3{,}600 + 6{,}400 = 10{,}000 = c^2$. So to find c, we take the square root of 10,000, which is 100 feet.

Session 3. Open-response Question

41 A sum of money is deposited in a bank account, where it earns 10% interest per year. No other deposits or withdrawals are made. After 3 years, the account holds $798.60.

   a. How much was in the bank account originally? Show your work.

41a. **$600.** Let's think about it this way: Some amount in the bank account after the second year plus 10% equals $798.60, the amount after the third year. What was the amount after the second year? We can write an equation $x + \dfrac{10}{100}x = 798.60$, or $1.1x = 798.60$. If we solve for x, we get $x = 726$. This amount was, in turn, 10% more than was there after the first year. So we can repeat the process: $1.1x = 726$. So after the first year there was $660. Finally, we can do it once more to see how much was originally there. If we solve $1.1x = 660$, we get $600.

   b. After how many years will the amount of money in the account be more than $1,000? Show your work.

41b. **6 years.** If we increase the value of the account by 10% per year, this is the same as multiplying the value in the account by 1.1. So after 4 years the value will be 1.1×798.60 (we were already told that this is the total after 3 years), which is $878.46. After 5 years it will be equal to $966.31. After 6 years, it will be $1,062.94.

   c. Write a mathematical expression to show how much money will be in the account after any given number of years.

41c. $x \times (1.1)^y$. Since the value increases by 1.1 times the original amount every year, we can write a general equation $x \times (1.1)^y$ where x is the original value of the account and y is the number of years.

42. A Worcester auto dealership pays $34,000 in rent and other general expenses every month. Furthermore, this dealership buys their cars for $15,550 and sells them for $16,400. The owner of the dealership, Gil, thinks that he needs to sell 50 cars every month to break even.

42. Gil is not a very bright businessman. His calculations are wrong, and we're going to show you why

   a. Is Gil correct in his estimation that he needs to sell 50 cars per month to break even? If he was wrong, what was the right answer? Show how you found your result.

a. If Gil is buying his cars for $15,550 and selling them for $16,400, then he is making a profit of $850 per car. If he needs to pay off $34,000 in rent and other expenses each month, you can simply divide 34,000 by 850 to figure out how many cars he needs to sell to break even. The answer is 40, not 50.

   b. If the rent of the auto dealership went up $2,720 per month, how many cars would Gil need to sell to make a profit in a month? Explain how you found your answer.

b. Instead of dividing $34,000 by $850, now you just have to divide $36,720 (the original expenses plus $2,720) by $850. The answer, 43.2, tells you how many cars Gil needs to sell to break even. But the questions asked how many he needed to sell to make a profit. So the answer is 44.

   c. Gil decides that he needs to create a formula to help him figure out his monthly losses or profits. Write a formula to help Gil determine his monthly losses or profits, using the variables listed below.

   - Rent and other expenses: R
   - Buying cost for the dealership to buy each car: B
   - Selling price for each car: S
   - Number of cars sold in a month: N
   - Profit or loss per month: P

c. You already know this equation if you got either parts a or b correct. But it can get confusing, so we'll show you how to arrange the variables in a correct equation.

   We know that Gil makes money on the difference between buying and selling the cars in his dealership. That equation can be represented as $S - B$. Therefore, the total amount of money that Gil makes is represented by the number of cars he sells (N) multiplied by the difference between buying and selling his cars ($S - B$). That part of the equation is $N(S - B)$. The profit (P) is found by subtracting the rent and other expenses (R) from $N(S - B)$. Your final answer should look like this:

   $$P = R - N(S - B) \qquad or$$

   $$R - N(S - B) = P.$$

Chapter 10

Practice Test 2

Values of Trigonometric Functions

Angle	Sin	Cos	Tan	Angle	Sin	Cos	Tan
1°	0.0175	0.9998	0.0175	46°	0.7193	0.6947	1.0355
2°	0.0349	0.9994	0.0349	47°	0.7314	0.6820	1.0724
3°	0.0523	0.9986	0.0524	48°	0.7431	0.6691	1.1106
4°	0.0698	0.9976	0.0699	49°	0.7547	0.6561	1.1504
5°	0.0872	0.9962	0.0875	50°	0.7660	0.6428	1.1918
6°	0.1045	0.9945	0.1051	51°	0.7771	0.6293	1.2349
7°	0.1219	0.9925	0.1227	52°	0.7880	0.6157	1.2799
8°	0.1392	0.9903	0.1405	53°	0.7986	0.6018	1.3270
9°	0.1564	0.9877	0.1584	54°	0.8090	0.5878	1.3764
10°	0.1736	0.9848	0.1763	55°	0.8192	0.5736	1.4281
11°	0.1908	0.9816	0.1944	56°	0.8290	0.5592	1.4826
12°	0.2079	0.9781	0.2126	57°	0.8387	0.5446	1.5399
13°	0.2250	0.9744	0.2309	58°	0.8480	0.5299	1.6003
14°	0.2419	0.9703	0.2493	59°	0.8572	0.5150	1.6643
15°	0.2588	0.9659	0.2679	60°	0.8660	0.5000	1.7321
16°	0.2756	0.9613	0.2867	61°	0.8746	0.4848	1.8040
17°	0.2924	0.9563	0.3057	62°	0.8829	0.4695	1.8807
18°	0.3090	0.9511	0.3249	63°	0.8910	0.4540	1.9626
19°	0.3256	0.9455	0.3443	64°	0.8988	0.4384	2.0503
20°	0.3420	0.9397	0.3640	65°	0.9063	0.4226	2.1445
21°	0.3584	0.9336	0.3839	66°	0.9135	0.4067	2.2460
22°	0.3746	0.9272	0.4040	67°	0.9205	0.3907	2.3559
23°	0.3907	0.9205	0.4245	68°	0.9272	0.3746	2.4751
24°	0.4067	0.9135	0.4452	69°	0.9336	0.3584	2.6051
25°	0.4226	0.9063	0.4663	70°	0.9397	0.3420	2.7475
26°	0.4384	0.8988	0.4877	71°	0.9455	0.3256	2.9042
27°	0.4540	0.8910	0.5095	72°	0.9511	0.3090	3.0777
28°	0.4695	0.8829	0.5317	73°	0.9563	0.2924	3.2709
29°	0.4848	0.8746	0.5543	74°	0.9613	0.2756	3.4874
30°	0.5000	0.8660	0.5774	75°	0.9659	0.2588	3.7321
31°	0.5150	0.8572	0.6009	76°	0.9703	0.2419	4.0108
32°	0.5299	0.8480	0.6249	77°	0.9744	0.2250	4.3315
33°	0.5446	0.8387	0.6494	78°	0.9781	0.2079	4.7046
34°	0.5592	0.8290	0.6745	79°	0.9816	0.1908	5.1446
35°	0.5736	0.8192	0.7002	80°	0.9848	0.1736	5.6713
36°	0.5878	0.8090	0.7265	81°	0.9877	0.1564	6.3138
37°	0.6018	0.7986	0.7536	82°	0.9903	0.1392	7.1154
38°	0.6157	0.7880	0.7813	83°	0.9925	0.1219	8.1443
39°	0.6293	0.7771	0.8098	84°	0.9945	0.1045	9.5144
40°	0.6428	0.7660	0.8391	85°	0.9962	0.0872	11.4301
41°	0.6561	0.7547	0.8693	86°	0.9976	0.0698	14.3007
42°	0.6691	0.7431	0.9004	87°	0.9986	0.0523	19.0811
43°	0.6820	0.7314	0.9325	88°	0.9994	0.0349	28.6363
44°	0.6947	0.7193	0.9657	89°	0.9998	0.0175	57.2900
45°	0.7071	0.7071	1.0000	90°	1.0000	0.0000	------

Formula Sheet

<u>Volume Formulas</u>

cube............$V = e^3$

cylinder.........$V = \pi r^2 h$

cone...........$V = \dfrac{1}{3}\pi r^2 h$

regular prism......$V = Bh$ (B = area of the base)

sphere..........$V = \dfrac{4}{3}\pi r^3$

<u>Area Formulas</u>

triangle..........$A = \dfrac{1}{2}bh$

rectangle.........$A = bh$

square...........$A = s^2$

triangle..........$A = \dfrac{1}{2}h(b_1 + b_2)$

<u>Circle Formulas</u>

$C = 2\pi r$

$A = \pi r^2$

<u>Surface Area Formulas</u>

sphere..........$SA = 4\pi r^2$

cube............$SA = 6e^2$

cylinder.........$SA = 2\pi r^2 + 2\pi rh$

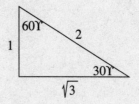

Final tips on the practice tests:

Give yourself no more than 45 minutes to complete each session. Either set an alarm or have a parent or a friend tell you when your time is up.

You are not allowed to use your calculator for the first session.

Remember that although the actual Grade 10 MCAS Math test has 42 scored questions, you will see about seven additional questions throughout the exam. These questions are called field-test (or matrix) items, and they're being tested for future exams. They won't count toward your score, but since you won't know which questions are the matrix items, you'll have to answer every question as if it counts.

Session 1, Multiple-choice Questions

(No calculator allowed)

1   Which of the following is equivalent to $\dfrac{16}{25}$?

A. .32

B. .64

C. 3.2

D. 6.4

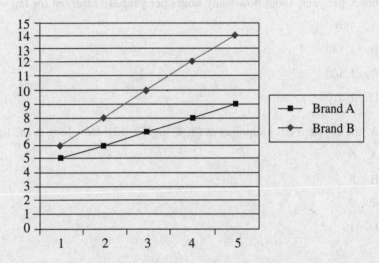

2   The graph above shows the prices of 2 brands of batteries. If these rates remain the same, how much more will 10 batteries of Brand B cost than 10 batteries of Brand A?

A. $6

B. $8

C. $9

D. $10

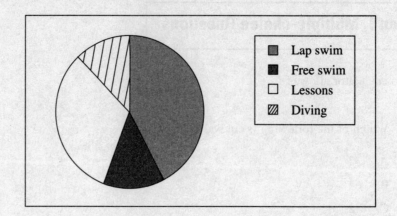

	Lap swim
	Free swim
	Lessons
	Diving

3   The chart above shows the daily schedule for the Smithtown pool. If the pool is open 3,120 hours per year, about how many hours per year are reserved for lap swimming?

A. 780

B. 1,340

C. 1,560

D. 1,610

4   A line segment has endpoints at (3, 4) and (9, 12). How long is the line segment?

A. 6

B. 8

C. 9

D. 10

5   For a science experiment, Mandy measures how fast her heart beats while she runs on a treadmill at different speeds. The following shows the number of beats per minute of Mandy's heart at various speeds.

Running speed	Beats per minute
2 mph	90
4 mph	100
6 mph	108
8 mph	102

Which of the following graphs best shows the number of heartbeats per minute with respect to speed?

A.
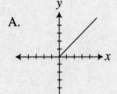

C.
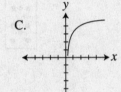

B.
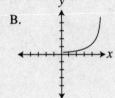

D.
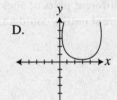

6   Which of the following will give a negative even result?

A. A negative odd number multiplied by a positive odd number

B. A negative even number multiplied by a positive odd number

C. A negative even number multiplied by a negative even number

D. A negative odd number multiplied by a negative odd number

7   Which of the following forms could be folded to create a cube where the sum of the numbers on the opposing faces is always 7?

A.
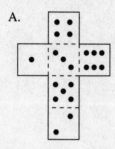

C.
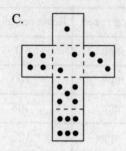

B.
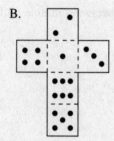

D.
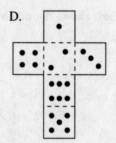

8   John needs to pick his clothes for the day. He can choose from 6 different shirts, 4 different pairs of pants, and 8 different pairs of socks. If he chooses 1 shirt, 1 pair of pants, and 1 pair of socks, how many different outfits could he choose?

A. 24

B. 48

C. 192

D. 224

9 $\dfrac{\sqrt{64^1}}{8^1} =$

   A. $\dfrac{1}{2}$

   B. 1

   C. 4

   D. 8

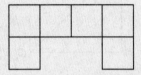

10 The figure above is composed of 6 equal squares. If the perimeter of the figure is 56 cm, what is its area?

   A. 16 cm²

   B. 42 cm²

   C. 66 cm²

   D. 96 cm²

11   On her first 3 math tests, Sylvia averaged 87 points. What must she score on her fourth test in order to have an average of 89?

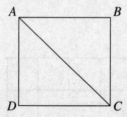

12   If the square above has an area of 10, what is the length of *AC*?

Session 1, Open-response Question

13 Ten slips of paper, numbered 1 to 10, are placed into a hat.

    a. If Alex draws out 1 slip of paper at random, what is the chance that the number on that slip is a multiple of 2?

    b. If the first slip of paper Alex draws out is the number 8, what is the chance that the next slip she draws out will have a number greater than 5? Show your work.

    c. How many slips of paper would Alex need to draw in order to be certain to draw a slip with an odd number on it?

Session 1, Short-answer Questions

14 Jamie has a jar of marbles. 20% of the marbles are blue, and the rest are red. 15% of the marbles are plastic, and the rest are metal. If Jamie selects 1 marble at random from the jar, what is the probability that it will be red and made of metal?

15 Based on the following chart, how many gears can be made in 13 days?

Days of Work	1	2	3	4	—	13
Gears made	85	170	255	340	—	?

16 Two ordinary 6-sided number cubes, with sides numbered 1 to 6, are thrown once.

   a. What is the probability that the sum of their faces will equal 7? Show your work.

   b. Draw the sample space.

17 A merchant can sell 300 pounds of fish for $800. At this rate, how much would 26 pounds of fish cost?

A. $69.33

B. $72.66

C. $83.25

D. $92.30

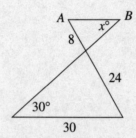

18 In the figure above, $x = 30°$. What is the length of AB?

A. 10

B. 12

C. 18

D. 22

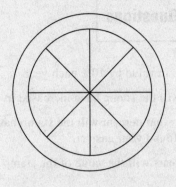

19 The wheel above has an area of 36π inches. If the wheel does not slip, how far will it have

traveled after $4\frac{1}{2}$ revolutions?

A. 12π inches

B. 48π inches

C. 54π inches

D. 60π inches

20 How many cereal boxes with dimensions $2 \times 1 \times 1$ can fit into a carton of dimensions $8 \times 8 \times 8$?

A. 32

B. 128

C. 256

D. 512

21 A rare stamp increases in value by 10% each year.

  a. By what percent will the stamp have increased in value after 2 years?

  b. By approximately what percent will the stamp have increased in value after 4 years? Explain how you found your answer.

  c. After how many years will the value of the stamp double? Explain how you found your answer.

	A	B	C	D
1	2	3	4	5
2	4	9	16	25
3	8	27	64	125
4	16	81	256	525
5				

22 Jason has created a spreadsheet in which he has placed the powers of 2, 3, 4 and 5.

  a. What numbers will appear in the 5th row?

  b. Jason proposes that any number in column C will be found in column A. Is Jason correct? Explain your reasoning.

Session 3, Multiple-choice Questions

n	3	4	5	6
$f(n)$	11	20	31	44

23 Which of the following formulas gives the correct formula for $f(n)$?

A. $n^2 + n$

B. $n(n + 2) - 4$

C. $3n + 2$

D. $n(n + 3) + 3$

24 Which of the following sets does NOT have a median of 85?

A. 85, 95, 84, 96, 83

B. 91, 87, 66, 83, 51, 90

C. 89, 89, 81, 81

D. 94, 85, 94, 67, 11, 86

25 If a coin is tossed 3 times, what is the probability that it will come up "heads" 3 times in a row?

A. $\frac{1}{8}$

B. $\frac{1}{4}$

C. $\frac{1}{3}$

D. $\frac{1}{2}$

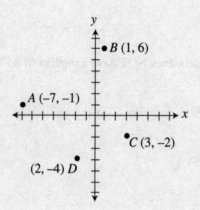

26 In the figure above, which of the following points is on the line $2y - 4x = 8$?

A. Point A

B. Point B

C. Point C

D. Point D

27 A statement is made that for all values n, n is rational when n^2 is rational. Which of the following values for n shows that this statement is not always true?

   A. $n = 103$

   B. $n = \sqrt{10}$

   C. $n = 0$

   D. $n = -2$

28 Which of the following will be negative for $x = 5$?

   A. $f(x) = 3x - x^1$

   B. $f(x) = 3x - x^2$

   C. $f(x) = 5x - 20$

   D. $f(x) = -x + 10$

29 In the formula $q = \dfrac{x^2}{2}$, if the value of x is doubled, then the value of q:

   A. increases by 400%

   B. increases by 25%

   C. decreases 25%

   D. does not change

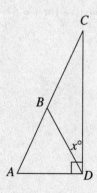

30 In the figure above $AB = BD = AD$. What is the value of $x°$?

   A. 30°

   B. 50°

   C. 60°

   D. 70°

31 If $15 > x > -5$, and $8 > y > 3$, which of the following gives the range of possible values of $x + y$?

A. $7 > x + y > -2$

B. $7 > x + y > 2$

C. $23 > x + y > -2$

D. $23 > x + y > 2$

32 What is the slope of the line that is perpendicular to the line that passes through points $(-1, 3)$ and $(1, 2)$?

A. $-\dfrac{1}{2}$

B. $\dfrac{1}{2}$

C. 1

D. -1

33 Alex's brother promises Alex, "If you win the match, then I will eat my hat." Which of the following would show that Alex's brother did not keep his promise?

A. Alex does not win the match, and his brother does not eat his hat.

B. Alex does not win the match, and his brother eats his hat.

C. Alex wins the match, and his brother does not eat his hat.

D. Alex wins the match, and his brother eats his hat.

34 A baker makes pies in the following order: cherry, apple, blueberry, lemon, rhubarb, blackberry, strawberry. If he then begins again with cherry, what is the flavor of the 87th pie?

A. Blueberry

B. Lemon

C. Rhubarb

D. Blackberry

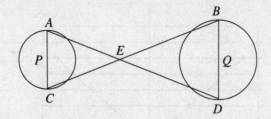

35 An astronomer wishes to know the diameter of Planet *Q*. He knows the diameter of Planet *P*, shown as line *AC*, and wants to figure out the diameter of Planet *Q*, shown as line *BD*. The diameter of Planet *P* is 10,000 meters, and point *E* is one-third of the distance from the center of Planet *P* to the center of Planet *Q*. If the distance from *A* to *D* is the same as the distance from *B* to *C*, what is the diameter of Planet *Q*?

A. 5,000 meters

B. 15,000 meters

C. 20,000 meters

D. 30,000 meters

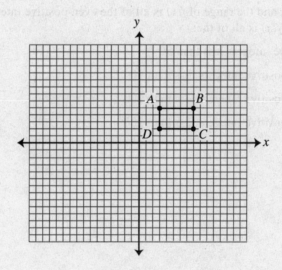

36 If the figure above is translated 3 points up and then reflected across the *x*-axis, what will be the coordinates of point *B*?

A. (–8, 8)

B. (8, –8)

C. (8, 5)

D. (8, –5)

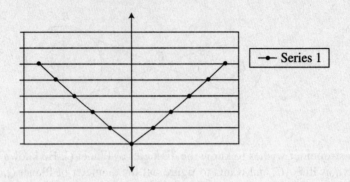

37 Which of the following equations could describe the figure above?

  A. $y = 50 - x^2$

  B. $y = |x| - 3$

  C. $y = 4x^2$

  D. $y = 3x + 5$

38 If $f(x) = 2x$ and the range of $f(x)$ is all of the even positive integers less than 100, then the domain of $f(x)$ is all of the:

  A. positive integers less than 50

  B. even positive integers less than 50

  C. even positive integers less than 100

  D. even positive integers less than 200

39 The ratio of the volume of a cylinder with diameter h and height h to the volume of a cube with side h is:

A. greater than 1

B. less than 1

C. equal to 1

D. cannot be determined from the information given

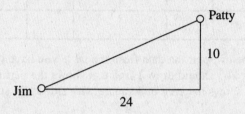

40 Jim kicks a ball in a straight line from the ground up to his friend Patty, who is in a tree at a point 10 feet above the ground. If the base of the tree Patty is in is 24 feet away from Jim, how far does the ball travel?

A. 20 feet

B. 26 feet

C. 30 feet

D. 36 feet

41 a. Create a chart showing, for the following values of s, the perimeter and area of a square with side s.

s	1	2	3	4	5
Perim.					
Area					

b. On the graph below, plot the data from the table you have just created, using the x-axis for the values of s. You should draw 1 line that shows the perimeter of a square with side s, and 1 line that shows the area of a square with side s. Be sure to show where these 2 lines intersect.

c. Give a formula for deriving the area (A) of a square given its perimeter (P).

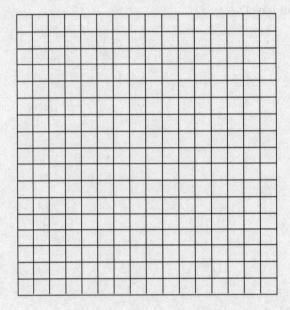

42 A stock is bought for $100,000. The value of this stock changes according to the following schedule.

- The value of the stock falls 50% during the first year.

- After the first year, the value of the stock rises 10% every year.

a. What is the value of the stock after five years? Show how you found your answer.

b. During which year is the value of the stock worth more than $100,000? Show or explain how you found your answer.

c. Suppose there was second stock that was bought for $100,000. Its value dropped 70% in the first year. Then it rose 20% every year after that. Which stock would be worth more after six years? Show all your work.

Practice Test 2
Answers and Explanations

1   Which of the following is equivalent to $\frac{16}{25}$?

A.   .32

B.   .64

C.   3.2

D.   6.4

1   B   The easiest way to solve this is to convert $\frac{16}{25}$ into decimal. If we multiply the top and bottom by 4, we can see that $\frac{16}{25}$ is equal to $\frac{64}{100}$, which the same as .64. That's **B**.

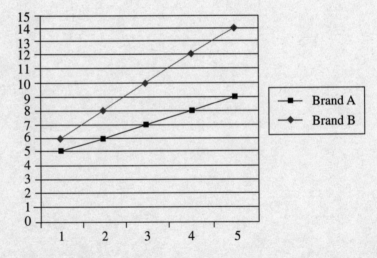

2   The graph above shows the prices of 2 brands of batteries. If these rates remain the same, how much more will 10 batteries of Brand B cost than 10 batteries of Brand A?

A. $6

B. $8

C. $9

D. $10

2 D According to the chart, Brand A increases by $1 for each successive unit, so 10 units will cost $14. Brand B increases by $2 for each successive unit, so 10 units will cost $24.

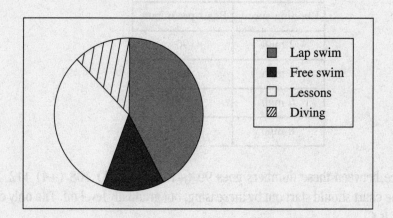

Session 3:

23	B
24	D
25	A
26	B
27	B
28	B
29	A
30	A
31	C
32	D
33	C
34	A
35	C
36	B
37	B
38	A
39	B
40	B

3 The chart above shows the daily schedule for the Smithtown pool. If the pool is open 3,120 hours per year, about how many hours per year are reserved for lap swimming?

   A. 780

   B. 1,340

   C. 1,560

   D. 1,610

3 B According to the chart, the amount of time allocated to lap swimming is somewhat less than half, but more than a quarter, of the total hours. Since the total hours are 3,120, the number allocated to lap swimming must be bigger than 780, but less than 1,560. Look at the answer choices—it has to be **B**.

4 A line segment has endpoints at (3, 4) and (9, 12). How long is the line segment?

   A. 6

   B. 8

   C. 9

   D. 10

4 D The easiest way to find this distance is to make a right triangle that connects these two points. If we do, we find that one leg of the right triangle has length 6 and the other has length 8. You can use the Pythagorean theorem, but if you've memorized your ratios, you'll know that 6:8:10 is one of them. So the hypotenuse (which is the distance between the two points) is equal to 10.

5   For a science experiment, Mandy measures how fast her heart beats while she runs on a treadmill at different speeds. The following shows the number of beats per minute of Mandy's heart at various speeds.

Running speed	Beats per minute
2 mph	90
4 mph	100
6 mph	108
8 mph	102

5   C The difference between these numbers goes 90 (+10) 100 (+8) 108 (+4) 112. This means that the chart should start out by increasing, but gradually level off. The only chart that does this is **C**.

6   Which of the following will give a negative even result?

A.   A negative odd number multiplied by a positive odd number

B.   A negative even number multiplied by a positive odd number

C.   A negative even number multiplied by a negative even number

D.   A negative odd number multiplied by a negative odd number

6   B Let's use POE to disprove the answer choices. Let's try choice **A**. A negative odd times a positive odd gives a negative odd: for example, $-3 \times 3 = -9$. How about choice **B**? A negative even times a positive odd—such as $-4 \times 3 = -12$—gives a negative even result, which is what we're looking for.

7 Which of the following forms could be folded to create a cube where the sum of the numbers on the opposing faces is always 7?

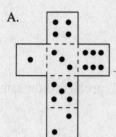

A.

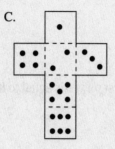

C.

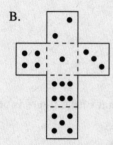

B.

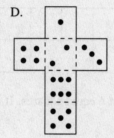

D.

7 **D** Use those answer choices! In choice **A**, the sides with numbers 2 and 5, as well as the sides with 3 and 4, are not facing each other. In choice **B**, the sides with numbers 2 and 5 as well as the sides with 6 and 1 are not facing each other. In choice **C**, the sides with numbers 2 and 5 are not facing each other.

8 John needs to pick his clothes for the day. He can choose from 6 different shirts, 4 different pairs of pants, and 8 different pairs of socks. If he chooses 1 shirt, 1 pair of pants, and 1 pair of socks, how many different outfits could he choose?

A. 24

B. 48

C. 192

D 224

8 **C** The number of different combinations John can create is equal to the product of the number of different things from which he has to choose. He has 6 shirts, 4 pairs of pants, and 8 pairs of socks to choose from, so he could choose $6 \times 4 \times 8$, or 192 different outfits.

9 $\dfrac{\sqrt{64^1}}{8^1} =$

    A. $\dfrac{1}{2}$

    B. 1

    C. 4

    D. 8

9 B Remember than anything to the first power is equal to itself, so this problem is the same as $\dfrac{\sqrt{64}}{8}$, which equals $\dfrac{8}{8}$, or 1.

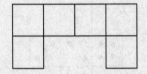

10 The figure above is composed of 6 equal squares. If the perimeter of the figure is 56 cm, what is its area?

    A. 16 cm^2

    B. 42 cm^2

    C. 66 cm^2

    D. 96 cm^2

10 D The perimeter of 56 is the sum of the sides of the figure. The figure has 14 equal sides, so each side must measure 4. Therefore, each square has an area of 16. This makes the total area of the figure equal to 6×16, or 96.

Session 1. Short-answer Questions

11   On her first 3 math tests, Sylvia averaged 87 points. What must she score on her fourth test in order to have an average of 89?

11   **95 points.** To get an average of 89 on four tests, Sylvia will need to score a total of 356 points on those four tests. If Sylvia averaged 87 points on her first 3 tests, the sum of her scores on those tests must have been 261. Therefore, on her fourth test she needs to score $356 - 261 = 95$ points.

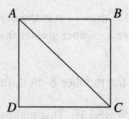

12   If the square above has an area of 10, what is the length of AC?

12   $\sqrt{20}$. If the area of the square is 10, then the base times the height must equal 10. In this case the base and the height are equal, so we can say that the length of 1 side squared must equal 10. What number times itself equals 10? $\sqrt{10}$. So each side is equal to $\sqrt{10}$. We also know that the diagonal AC is the hypotenuse of a right triangle with 2 sides equal to $\sqrt{10}$. We can use the Pythagorean theorem to find AC since we know that $AC^2 = \sqrt{10}^2 + \sqrt{10}^2$. So $AC^2 = 20$, and $AC = \sqrt{20}$.

13 Ten slips of paper, numbered 1 to 10, are placed into a hat.

    a.   If Alex draws out 1 slip of paper at random, what is the chance that the number on that slip is a multiple of 2?

13a. $\dfrac{1}{2}$. The multiples of 2 in the hat are 2, 4, 6, 8, and 10. So 5 of the 10 slips of paper are

multiples of 2. This means that if she draws 1 slip at random, she will have a $\dfrac{5}{10}$, or $\dfrac{1}{2}$

chance of drawing a slip with a multiple of 2.

    b.   If the first slip of paper Alex draws out is the number 8, what is the chance that the next slip she draws out will have a number greater than 5? Show your work.

13b. $\dfrac{4}{9}$. If she draws out the slip with the number 8 on it, the slips left in the hat are the slips

numbered 1, 2, 3, 4, 5, 6, 7, 9, and 10. This makes a total of 9 slips, of which 4 (the slips numbered 6, 7, 9, and 10) are greater than 5. Therefore, when she draws again,

she will have a $\dfrac{4}{9}$ chance of drawing a number greater than 5.

    c.   How many slips of paper would Alex need to draw in order to be certain to draw a slip with an odd number on it?

13c. This is not a question of probability, but one of certainty. To be absolutely certain of drawing a slip with an odd number, we have to rule out the worst possible case: It is possible that by chance she draws the 2, 4, 6, 8, and 10 slips before any others. To be absolutely sure that she draws an odd number, she will need to exhaust the even-numbered slips and then draw one more. This means she will have to draw 6 slips to be sure of getting an odd number.

Session 1. Short-answer Questions

14 Jamie has a jar of marbles. 20% of the marbles are blue, and the rest are red. 15% of the marbles are plastic, and the rest are metal. If Jamie selects 1 marble at random from the jar, what is the probability that it will be red and made of metal?

14 **68%.** Since 20% of the marbles are blue and the rest are red, we know that 80% of the marbles are red. The probability of picking a red marble is therefore .8. Likewise, we can figure out that 85% of the marbles are made of metal. The probability of picking a metal marble is therefore .85. The probability of picking a red metal marble is the product of these 2 probabilities, or .8 × .85 = .68, or a 68% chance.

15 Based on the following chart, how many gears can be made in 13 days?

Days of Work	1	2	3	4	—	13
Gears made	85	170	255	340	—	?

15 **1,105.** If we look at the pattern, it goes: 85 (+85) 170 (+85) 255 (+85) 239 . . . . So it appears to increase by 85 each time. If we extend this pattern out to the 13th day, we get 1,105.

16 Two ordinary 6-sided number cubes, with sides numbered 1 to 6, are thrown once.

    a.   What is the probability that the sum of their faces will equal 7? Show your work.

16a. $\dfrac{1}{6}$. There are 36 ways that we could roll the dice, of which 6 have a sum of 7. Therefore, the

        probability will be $\dfrac{6}{36}$, or $\dfrac{1}{6}$.

    b.   Draw the sample space.

16b.

	1	2	3	4	5	6
1	2	3	4	5	6	7
2	3	4	5	6	7	8
3	4	5	6	7	8	9
4	5	6	7	8	9	10
5	6	7	8	9	10	11
6	7	8	9	10	11	12

17 A merchant can sell 300 pounds of fish for $800. At this rate, how much would 26 pounds of fish cost?

   A. $69.33

   B. $72.66

   C. $83.25

   D. $92.30

17 A To solve this problem we can set up a proportion: $\dfrac{300}{\$800} = \dfrac{26}{x}$. If we cross-multiply and solve, we get $x = \$69.33$. That's **A**.

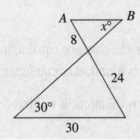

18 In the figure above, $x = 30°$. What is the length of AB?

   A. 10

   B. 12

   C. 18

   D. 22

18 A Since the triangles each have one angle of 30 degrees and another angle of the same measure (since a pair of angles are vertical angles and, therefore, have the same measurement) these triangles must be similar. Therefore, each side of one triangle is proportional to a corresponding side of the other triangle. The side opposite the 30-degree angle in the larger triangle measures 24; the side opposite the 30-degree angle in the smaller triangle measures 8. This tells us that each side of the larger triangle is 3 times as large as its corresponding side on the smaller triangle. This means that AB will be one-third as large as 30, or 10, choice **A**.

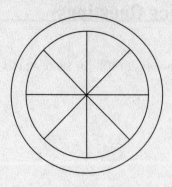

19 The wheel above has an area of 36π inches. If the wheel does not slip, how far will it have

traveled after $4\frac{1}{2}$ revolutions?

   A. 12π inches

   B. 48π inches

   C. 54π inches

   D. 60π inches

19 C In 1 revolution, a wheel will travel a distance equal to its circumference. If the wheel has
an area of 36π, then its radius is 6, and its circumference is 12π. So it will travel 12π in

1 revolution. Therefore, in $4\frac{1}{2}$ revolutions, it will travel 54π inches, choice **C**.

20 How many cereal boxes with dimensions $2 \times 1 \times 1$ can fit into a carton of dimensions $8 \times 8 \times 8$?

   A. 32

   B. 128

   C. 256

   D. 512

20 C The volume of a box $2 \times 1 \times 1$ is 2, and the volume of a carton $8 \times 8 \times 8$ is 512.
Therefore, we can fit $512 \div 2$, or 256 boxes inside the carton. That's **C**.

Session 2. Open-response Questions

21 A rare stamp increases in value by 10% each year.

    a.   By what percent will the stamp have increased in value after 2 years?

21a. **21%.** Let's assume that the original price of the stamp is $100 because plugging in 100 is always a good idea on percent questions. After 1 year, it will increase by 10% of $100, or $10. Its new price will be $110. After 2 years, it will increase another 10%. This time it will increase by 10% of $110, which is $11. Its new price will therefore be $121. After 2 years it has increased from $100 to $121, an increase of 21%.

    b.   By approximately what percent will the stamp have increased in value after 4 years? Explain how you found your answer.

21b. **46%.** If after 2 years the stamp is $121, then after the 3rd year it will increase by 10% of $121, which is $12.10. The price will increase to $133.10. After the 4th year it will increase by 10% of $133.10, which is the same as $13.31. So after 4 years, the price will be $146.41, which is an increase of about 46% over the original price.

    c.   After how many years will the value of the stamp double? Explain how you found your answer.

21c. **8 years.** Let's keep increasing the value of the stamp by 10%, which is the same thing as multiplying by 1.1. After 5 years, the price will be $161.05. After 6 years, it will be $177.16. After 7 years, it will be $194.88. So after the 8th year, it will be over $200 and will have more than doubled.

	A	B	C	D
1	2	3	4	5
2	4	9	16	25
3	8	27	64	125
4	16	81	256	525
5				

22 Jason has created a spreadsheet in which he has placed the powers of 2, 3, 4 and 5.

    a. What numbers will appear in the 5th row?

22a. The next powers of 2, 3, 4 and 5 will be 32, 243, 1,024, and 2,625.

    b. Jason proposes that any number in column C will be found in column A. Is Jason correct? Explain your reasoning.

22b. Jason is correct. Column A begins with the number 2, and each entry in the column is twice the previous entry. This means that the numbers in column A are equal to the powers of 2 (2^2, 2^3, 2^4, etc.). Column C begins with the number 4, and each entry in the column is 4 times the previous entry. This means that the numbers in column C are the powers of 4 (4^2, 4^3, 4^4, etc.). All of the powers of 4 are also powers of 2, as we can see from the fact that if we square any number in column A, we get the corresponding number in column C. So any number in column C will also appear in column A.

n	3	4	5	6
$f(n)$	11	20	31	44

23 Which of the following formulas gives the correct formula for $f(n)$?

A. $n^2 + n$

B. $n(n + 2) - 4$

C. $3n + 2$

D. $n(n + 3) + 3$

23 B If we plug in 3 for n, the formulas in choices **A** and **D** do not give us 11, so we can eliminate them. When we plug in 4 for n, choice **C** does not give us 20, so it can also be eliminated. That leaves **B**.

24 Which of the following sets does NOT have a median of 85?

A. 85, 95, 84, 96, 83

B. 91, 87, 66, 83, 51, 90

C. 89, 89, 81, 81

D. 94, 85, 94, 67, 11, 86

24 D If we put the numbers in choice **A** in ascending order, they are: 83, 84, 85, 95, 96. The median for this choice is 85, so we can eliminate it. For choice **B**, the numbers in order are: 51, 66, 83, 87, 90, 91. The 2 numbers in the middle are 83 and 87, and their average is 85. So we can eliminate **B**. In choice **C** the two middle numbers are 81 and 89, and their average is 85. For choice **D**, the numbers are: 11, 67, 85, 86, 94, 94. The 2 middle numbers here are 85 and 86, and their average is 85.5. So **D** is the answer.

25 If a coin is tossed 3 times, what is the probability that it will come up "heads" 3 times in a row?

A. $\dfrac{1}{8}$

B. $\dfrac{1}{4}$

C. $\dfrac{1}{3}$

D. $\dfrac{1}{2}$

25 A For each toss of the coin there is a $\dfrac{1}{2}$ chance that it will come up "heads." So the chance of getting "heads" 3 times in a row is $\dfrac{1}{2} \times \dfrac{1}{2} \times \dfrac{1}{2}$, or $\dfrac{1}{8}$.

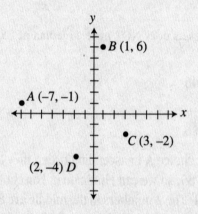

26 In the figure above, which of the following points is on the line $2y - 4x = 8$?

A. Point A

B. Point B

C. Point C

D. Point D

26 B The easiest way to solve this problem is to plug the x and y coordinates of each point into the equation and see which set of points makes it true. Point A is at $-7, -1$. If we plug -1 in for y and -7 in for x, the equation reads $2(-1) - 4(-7) = 8$. This is not true, so choice **A** can be eliminated. Let's try choice **B**. Does $2(6) - 4(1) = 8$? Yes.

27   A statement is made that for all values n, n is rational when n^2 is rational. Which of the following values for n shows that this statement is not always true?

   A. $n = 103$

   B. $n = \sqrt{10}$

   C. $n = 0$

   D. $n = -2$

27 B   Use POE. In **A**, **C**, and **D**, both n and n^2 will be rational. For choice **B**, n^2 is rational since it will be equal to 10, but n itself is not rational.

28   Which of the following will be negative for $x = 5$?

   A. $f(x) = 3x - x^1$

   B. $f(x) = 3x - x^2$

   C. $f(x) = 5x - 20$

   D. $f(x) = -x + 10$

28 B   Let's plug 5 into each function. Choice **A** gives us $15 - 5$, or 10. Choice **B** gives us $15 - 25$, or -10. That's negative, so that's the answer.

29   In the formula $q = \dfrac{x^2}{2}$, if the value of x is doubled, then the value of q:

   A. increases by 400%

   B. increases by 25%

   C. decreases 25%

   D. does not change

29 A   Let's plug in some numbers. If x begins at 4, then q will equal 8. If x doubles to 8, then q becomes 32. So the value of q has increased by 400%.

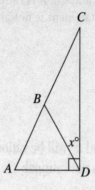

30 In the figure above $AB = BD = AD$. What is the value of $x°$?

A. 30°

B. 50°

C. 60°

D. 70°

30 A Since $AB = BD = AD$, we know that triangle ABD is equilateral, and each of its angles must be equal to 60 degrees. Since angle A equals 60 degrees, and triangle ACD is a right triangle, we know that the angle at C must equal 30 degrees. The angle CBD plus 60 degrees must equal 180 degrees, so it must be equal to 120 degrees. We have thus determined that the triangle BCD has 1 angle that equals 30 degrees, 1 angle that equals 120 degrees, and x. Therefore, x must equal 30 degrees.

31 If $15 > x > -5$, and $8 > y > 3$, which of the following gives the range of possible values of $x + y$?

A. $7 > x + y > -2$

B. $7 > x + y > 2$

C. $23 > x + y > -2$

D. $23 > x + y > 2$

31 C We know that x could be almost as small as -5, and y could be almost as small as 3, so the smallest value of $x + y$ will be something bigger than -2. Likewise, the biggest values of x and y are just less than 15 and 8, so their sum could be something just less than 23.

32 What is the slope of the line that is perpendicular to the line that passes through points (–1, 3) and (1, 2)?

A. $-\dfrac{1}{2}$

B. $\dfrac{1}{2}$

C. 1

D. –1

32 D Let's figure out the slope of the line that passes through (–1, 3) and (1, 2). The rise is –1, and the run is equal to 2, so the slope of this line will be $-\dfrac{1}{2}$. The line that is perpendicular will have a slope equal to the negative reciprocal of $-\dfrac{1}{2}$, which is 2.

33 Alex's brother promises Alex, "If you win the match, then I will eat my hat." Which of the following would show that Alex's brother did not keep his promise?

A. Alex does not win the match, and his brother does not eat his hat.

B. Alex does not win the match, and his brother eats his hat.

C. Alex wins the match, and his brother does not eat his hat.

D. Alex wins the match, and his brother eats his hat.

33 C An if . . . then statement is shown to be false when the IF part is true, but the THEN part is false. So we're looking for a statement that says that Alex does win the match, but his brother does not eat his hat.

34 A baker makes pies in the following order: cherry, apple, blueberry, lemon, rhubarb, blackberry, strawberry. If he then begins again with cherry, what is the flavor of the 87th pie?

A. Blueberry

B. Lemon

C. Rhubarb

D. Blackberry

34 A Start writing the series out longhand until you see the pattern. The 7th pie will be strawberry, as will the 14th. This means that every 7th pie will be strawberry, including the 70th, the 77th, and the 84th. So the 85th will be cherry, the 86th will be apple, and the 87th will be blueberry.

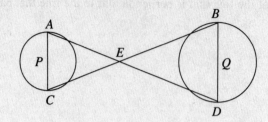

35 An astronomer wishes to know the diameter of Planet Q. He knows the diameter of Planet P, shown as line AC, and wants to figure out the diameter of Planet Q, shown as line BD. The diameter of Planet P is 10,000 meters, and point E is one-third of the distance from the center of Planet P to the center of Planet Q. If the distance from A to D is the same as the distance from B to C, what is the diameter of Planet Q?

    A. 5,000 meters

    B. 15,000 meters

    C. 20,000 meters

    D. 30,000 meters

35 C Since AD is equal to BC, and E is exactly one-third of the distance from the center of P to

the center of Q, the 2 triangles formed are similar. Further, since point E is $\dfrac{1}{3}$ the distance

from Planet P, it is $\dfrac{2}{3}$ the distance from Planet Q, and, therefore, 1 triangle is twice the size

of the other. So if AC is 10,000 meters long, then BD must be 20,000 meters long.

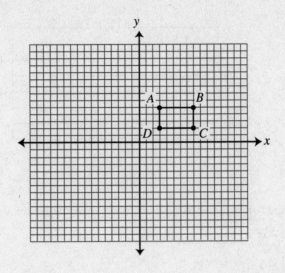

36 If the figure above is translated 3 points up and then reflected across the x-axis, what will be the coordinates of point B?

A. (–8, 8)

B. (8, –8)

C. (8, 5)

D. (8, –5)

36 B Point B is currently at (8, 5). When the figure is translated 3 points up, it will be at (8, 8). Then when the figure is reflected across the x-axis, it will be at (8, –8).

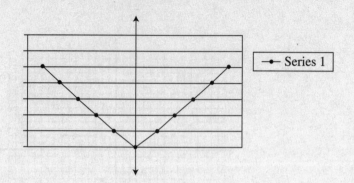

37 Which of the following equations could describe the figure above?

   A. $y = 50 - x^2$

   B. $y = |x| - 3$

   C. $y = 4x^2$

   D. $y = 3x + 5$

37 B The figure in question begins with large values of y, drops at a constant rate, and then rises again at a constant rate. Let's plug in the $-3, -2, -1, 0, 1, 2,$ and 3 for x in these functions and see how they would look:

x	−3	−2	−1	0	1	2	3
A	41	46	49	50	49	46	41
B	0	−1	−2	−3	−2	−1	0
C	36	16	4	0	4	16	36
D	−10	−1	2	5	8	11	14

Use POE! Choice **A** can be eliminated because it rises and then falls, which is backwards. Choice **D** can be eliminated because it continually rises. Between choices **B** and **C**, choice **B** is more accurate because it falls and rises at a constant rate (in a straight line).

38 If $f(x) = 2x$ and the range of $f(x)$ is all of the even positive integers less than 100, then the domain of $f(x)$ is all of the:

A. positive integers less than 50

B. even positive integers less than 50

C. even positive integers less than 100

D. even positive integers less than 200

38 A What numbers, if we plug them in for x, will generate all of the even positive integers less than 100? Let's try choice **A**. If we plug in the positive integers less than 50 (namely 1, 2, 3, 4 . . .) we find that f(x) = 2, 4, 6, 8 . . . which is exactly the result we need.

39 The ratio of the volume of a cylinder with diameter h and height h to the volume of a cube with side h is:

A. greater than 1

B. less than 1

C. equal to 1

D. cannot be determined from the information given

39 B

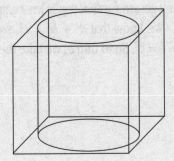

If you draw an accurate picture, you can probably do this one visually. A cylinder with diameter h and height h will fit inside a cube with side h because the face of the cylinder—a circle with diameter h—can be inscribed in the face of the cube, and the heights of the two are identical. Since the cylinder can fit inside the cube, and is therefore smaller than the cube, the ratio of the volume of the cylinder to the volume of the cube is less than 1.

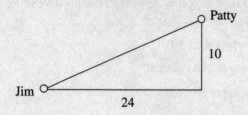

Patty

10

Jim

24

40 Jim kicks a ball in a straight line from the ground up to his friend Patty, who is in a tree at a point 10 feet above the ground. If the base of the tree Patty is in is 24 feet away from Jim, how far does the ball travel?

A. 20 feet

B. 26 feet

C. 30 feet

D. 36 feet

40 B You probably noticed that the flight of the ball goes along the hypotenuse of the right triangle with sides 10 and 24. Before we use the Pythagorean theorem, start by Ballparking! We know that the hypotenuse is bigger than the side of 24, so we can eliminate choice **A**; but it's not *too* much bigger than 24, so we can eliminate **D** as well. If you can't get any further, you at least can take a good guess. Now let's use the Pythagorean theorem. We know that $a^2 + b^2 = c^2$, so $10^2 + 24^2 = c^2$. If we calculate this out, we get $100 + 576 = 676 = c^2$. So to find c, we take the square root of 676, which is 26 feet.

41 a. Create a chart showing, for the following values of *s*, the perimeter and area of a square with side *s*.

s	1	2	3	4	5
Perim.					
Area					

41 a.

s	1	2	3	4	5	6
Perim.	4	8	12	16	20	24
Area	1	4	9	16	25	36

b. On the graph below, plot the data from the table you have just created, using the *x*-axis for the values of *s*. You should draw 1 line that shows the perimeter of a square with side *s*, and 1 line that shows the area of a square with side *s*. Be sure to show where these 2 lines intersect.

b.

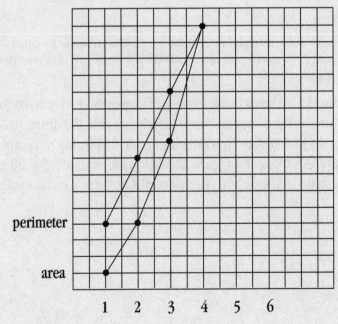

c. Give a formula for deriving the area (*A*) of a square given its perimeter (*P*).

c. $a = \left(\dfrac{p}{4}\right)^2$

42   A stock is bought for $100,000. The value of this stock changes according to the following schedule.

- The value of the stock falls 50% during the first year.

- After the first year, the value of the stock rises 10% every year.

42.   This problem can be tricky because the value of the stock decreases, then increases. But as long as you follow the value of the stock year-by-year, you'll be fine. Let's see how.

a.   What is the value of the stock after five years? Show how you found your answer.

a.   If the initial price of the stock is worth $100,000, then it would be worth $50,000 after one year (deducting 50%). Remember to get 10% of a number, you just multiply the number times .1. Add that number to the original figure to add 10%. After the first year, you add 10% to $50,000, which would equal $55,000. Adding 10% to that value, you get $60,500. So the stock is worth $60,500 after three years. After another year, it's worth $66,550. And after the fifth year, the value is $73,205.

b.   During which year is the value of the stock worth more than $100,000? Show or explain how you found your answer.

b.   You already know that the value of the stock is worth $73,205 after five years. Keep adding 10% to that figure until the total is over $100,000. After six years the total is $80,525.50. After seven years the total is $88,578.05. At the eight year the total is $97,435.86. So you can tell from this that the value of the stock will be more than $100,000 during the ninth year.

c.   Suppose there was second stock that was bought for $100,000. Its value dropped 70% in the first year. Then it rose 20% every year after that. Which stock would be worth more after six years? Show all your work.

c.   From the previous answer, you already know that the value of the original stock was worth $80,525.50 after six years. Now let's see what the second stock is worth. If it drops 70% after one year, then the value is $30,000. Add 20% and it's worth $36,000 after two years, $43,200 after three years, and $51.840 after four years. After five years, its value is $62,208. And after six years, the total value is $74,649.60. Therefore, the first stock is still worth more after six years.

Grade 10 MCAS Math Practice Test 1 Scoring Guide:

Session 1:

Multiple-choice Questions: 1–10   =   _____/10 points

Short-answer Questions: 11, 12, 14, 15   =   _____/4 points

Open-response Questions: 13, 16   =   _____/8 points

              _____/22 points

Session 2:

Multiple-choice Questions: 17–20   =   _____/4 points

Open-response Questions: 21, 22   =   _____/8 points

              _____/12 points

Session 3:

Multiple-choice Questions: 23–40   =   _____/18 points

Open-response Questions: 41, 42   =   _____/8 points

              _____/26 points

Session 1   =   _____/22 points

Session 2   =   _____/12 points

Session 3   =   _____/26 points

Total raw score for Practice Test #1   =   _____/60 points

To score your Open-response questions:

- Give yourself 4 points if your response showed a thorough understanding of the problem, and you answered all parts of the question correctly.

- Give yourself 3 points if your response showed a general understanding of the problem, and you answered most of the question correctly.

- Give yourself 2 points if your response showed a basic understanding of the problem, and you answered some of the question correctly.

- Give yourself 1 point if your response showed a minimal understanding of the problem.

- Give yourself 0 points if your response is completely incorrect, irrelevant to the concept being tested, or blank.

Raw Score to Scaled Score Conversion:

Total Raw Score	Scaled Score	Grade
53 or above	280	Pass/Advanced
52	278	Pass/Advanced
51	276	Pass/Advanced
50	274	Pass/Advanced
49	272	Pass/Advanced
48	268	Pass/Advanced
47	266	Pass/Advanced
46	264	Pass/Advanced
45	264	Pass/Advanced
44	260	Pass/Advanced
43	258	Pass/Proficient
42	256	Pass/Proficient
41	254	Pass/Proficient
40	250	Pass/Proficient
39	248	Pass/Proficient
38	248	Pass/Proficient
37	246	Pass/Proficient
36	244	Pass/Proficient
35	242	Pass/Proficient
34	240	Pass/Proficient
33	236	Pass/Proficient
32	234	Pass/Proficient
31	232	Pass/Proficient
30	230	Pass/Needs Improvement
29	228	Pass/Needs Improvement
28	226	Pass/Needs Improvement
27	226	Pass/Needs Improvement
26	224	Pass/Needs Improvement
25	222	Pass/Needs Improvement
24	220	Pass/Needs Improvement
23 or below	220	Failing

This scale is based on the 1999 Grade 10 MCAS Math exam. The conversion scale may change from year to year.

Grade 10 MCAS Math Practice Test 2 Scoring Guide:

Session 1:

Multiple-choice Questions: 1–10	=	_____/10 points
Short-answer Questions: 11, 12, 14, 15	=	_____/4 points
Open-response Questions: 13, 16	=	_____/8 points
		_____/22 points

Session 2:

Multiple-choice Questions: 17–20	=	_____/4 points
Open-response Questions: 21, 22	=	_____/8 points
		_____/12 points

Session 3:

Multiple-choice Questions: 23–40	=	_____/18 points
Open-response Questions: 41, 42	=	_____/8 points
		_____/26 points

Session 1	=	_____/22 points
Session 2	=	_____/12 points
Session 3	=	_____/26 points

Total raw score for Practice Test #2 = _____/60 points

To score your Open-response questions:

- Give yourself 4 points if your response showed a thorough understanding of the problem, and you answered all parts of the question correctly.

- Give yourself 3 points if your response showed a general understanding of the problem, and you answered most of the question correctly.

- Give yourself 2 points if your response showed a basic understanding of the problem, and you answered some of the question correctly.

- Give yourself 1 point if your response showed a minimal understanding of the problem.

- Give yourself 0 points if your response is completely incorrect, irrelevant to the concept being tested, or blank.

Raw Score to Scaled Score Conversion:

Total Raw Score	Scaled Score	Grade
53 or above	280	Pass/Advanced
52	278	Pass/Advanced
51	276	Pass/Advanced
50	274	Pass/Advanced
49	272	Pass/Advanced
48	268	Pass/Advanced
47	266	Pass/Advanced
46	264	Pass/Advanced
45	264	Pass/Advanced
44	260	Pass/Advanced
43	258	Pass/Proficient
42	256	Pass/Proficient
41	254	Pass/Proficient
40	250	Pass/Proficient
39	248	Pass/Proficient
38	248	Pass/Proficient
37	246	Pass/Proficient
36	244	Pass/Proficient
35	242	Pass/Proficient
34	240	Pass/Proficient
33	236	Pass/Proficient
32	234	Pass/Proficient
31	232	Pass/Proficient
30	230	Pass/Needs Improvement
29	228	Pass/Needs Improvement
28	226	Pass/Needs Improvement
27	226	Pass/Needs Improvement
26	224	Pass/Needs Improvement
25	222	Pass/Needs Improvement
24	220	Pass/Needs Improvement
23 or below	220	Failing

This scale is based on the 1999 Grade 10 MCAS Math exam. The conversion scale may change from year to year.

Completely darken bubbles with a No. 2 pencil. If you make a mistake, be sure to erase mark completely. Erase all stray marks.

1. YOUR NAME:
(Print) _____
Last   First   M.I.

SIGNATURE: _____ DATE: _____ / ___ /

HOME ADDRESS: _____
(Print)   Number

_____
City   State   Zip Code

PHONE NO.: _____
(Print)

IMPORTANT: Please fill in these boxes exactly as shown on the back cover of your test book.

2. TEST FORM

_____

6. DATE OF BIRTH

Month	Day		Year	
○ JAN				
○ FEB				
○ MAR	⓪	⓪	⓪	⓪
○ APR	①	①	①	①
○ MAY	②	②	②	②
○ JUN	③	③	③	③
○ JUL		④	④	④
○ AUG		⑤	⑤	⑤
○ SEP		⑦	⑦	⑦
○ OCT		⑧	⑧	⑧
○ NOV		⑨	⑨	⑨
○ DEC				

3. TEST CODE   4. REGISTRATION NUMBER

⓪	Ⓐ	⓪	⓪	⓪	⓪	⓪	⓪	⓪	⓪	⓪
①	Ⓑ	①	①	①	①	①	①	①	①	①
②	Ⓒ	②	②	②	②	②	②	②	②	②
③	Ⓓ	③	③	③	③	③	③	③	③	③
④	Ⓔ	④	④	④	④	④	④	④	④	④
⑤	Ⓕ	⑤	⑤	⑤	⑤	⑤	⑤	⑤	⑤	⑤
⑦	Ⓖ	⑦	⑦	⑦	⑦	⑦	⑦	⑦	⑦	⑦
⑧		⑧	⑧	⑧	⑧	⑧	⑧	⑧	⑧	⑧
⑨		⑨	⑨	⑨	⑨	⑨	⑨	⑨	⑨	⑨

7. SEX
○ MALE
○ FEMALE

The Princeton Review
© 1996 Princeton Review L.L.C.
FORM NO. 00001-PR

5. YOUR NAME

First 4 letters of last name				FIRST INIT	MID INIT
Ⓐ	Ⓐ	Ⓐ	Ⓐ	Ⓐ	Ⓐ
Ⓑ	Ⓑ	Ⓑ	Ⓑ	Ⓑ	Ⓑ
Ⓒ	Ⓒ	Ⓒ	Ⓒ	Ⓒ	Ⓒ
Ⓓ	Ⓓ	Ⓓ	Ⓓ	Ⓓ	Ⓓ
Ⓔ	Ⓔ	Ⓔ	Ⓔ	Ⓔ	Ⓔ
Ⓕ	Ⓕ	Ⓕ	Ⓕ	Ⓕ	Ⓕ
Ⓖ	Ⓖ	Ⓖ	Ⓖ	Ⓖ	Ⓖ
Ⓗ	Ⓗ	Ⓗ	Ⓗ	Ⓗ	Ⓗ
Ⓘ	Ⓘ	Ⓘ	Ⓘ	Ⓘ	Ⓘ
Ⓙ	Ⓙ	Ⓙ	Ⓙ	Ⓙ	Ⓙ
Ⓚ	Ⓚ	Ⓚ	Ⓚ	Ⓚ	Ⓚ
Ⓛ	Ⓛ	Ⓛ	Ⓛ	Ⓛ	Ⓛ
Ⓜ	Ⓜ	Ⓜ	Ⓜ	Ⓜ	Ⓜ
Ⓝ	Ⓝ	Ⓝ	Ⓝ	Ⓝ	Ⓝ
Ⓞ	Ⓞ	Ⓞ	Ⓞ	Ⓞ	Ⓞ
Ⓟ	Ⓟ	Ⓟ	Ⓟ	Ⓟ	Ⓟ
Ⓠ	Ⓠ	Ⓠ	Ⓠ	Ⓠ	Ⓠ
Ⓡ	Ⓡ	Ⓡ	Ⓡ	Ⓡ	Ⓡ
Ⓢ	Ⓢ	Ⓢ	Ⓢ	Ⓢ	Ⓢ
Ⓣ	Ⓣ	Ⓣ	Ⓣ	Ⓣ	Ⓣ
Ⓤ	Ⓤ	Ⓤ	Ⓤ	Ⓤ	Ⓤ
Ⓥ	Ⓥ	Ⓥ	Ⓥ	Ⓥ	Ⓥ
Ⓦ	Ⓦ	Ⓦ	Ⓦ	Ⓦ	Ⓦ
Ⓧ	Ⓧ	Ⓧ	Ⓧ	Ⓧ	Ⓧ
Ⓨ	Ⓨ	Ⓨ	Ⓨ	Ⓨ	Ⓨ
Ⓩ	Ⓩ	Ⓩ	Ⓩ	Ⓩ	Ⓩ

Practice Test ①

1. Ⓐ Ⓑ Ⓒ Ⓓ   15. Short-answer   29. Ⓐ Ⓑ Ⓒ Ⓓ
2. Ⓐ Ⓑ Ⓒ Ⓓ   16. Open-response   30. Ⓐ Ⓑ Ⓒ Ⓓ
3. Ⓐ Ⓑ Ⓒ Ⓓ   17. Ⓐ Ⓑ Ⓒ Ⓓ   31. Ⓐ Ⓑ Ⓒ Ⓓ
4. Ⓐ Ⓑ Ⓒ Ⓓ   18. Ⓐ Ⓑ Ⓒ Ⓓ   32. Ⓐ Ⓑ Ⓒ Ⓓ
5. Ⓐ Ⓑ Ⓒ Ⓓ   19. Ⓐ Ⓑ Ⓒ Ⓓ   33. Ⓐ Ⓑ Ⓒ Ⓓ
6. Ⓐ Ⓑ Ⓒ Ⓓ   20. Ⓐ Ⓑ Ⓒ Ⓓ   34. Ⓐ Ⓑ Ⓒ Ⓓ
7. Ⓐ Ⓑ Ⓒ Ⓓ   21. Open-response   35. Ⓐ Ⓑ Ⓒ Ⓓ
8. Ⓐ Ⓑ Ⓒ Ⓓ   22. Open-response   36. Ⓐ Ⓑ Ⓒ Ⓓ
9. Ⓐ Ⓑ Ⓒ Ⓓ   23. Ⓐ Ⓑ Ⓒ Ⓓ   37. Ⓐ Ⓑ Ⓒ Ⓓ
10. Ⓐ Ⓑ Ⓒ Ⓓ   24. Ⓐ Ⓑ Ⓒ Ⓓ   38. Ⓐ Ⓑ Ⓒ Ⓓ
11. Short-answer   25. Ⓐ Ⓑ Ⓒ Ⓓ   39. Ⓐ Ⓑ Ⓒ Ⓓ
12. Short-answer   26. Ⓐ Ⓑ Ⓒ Ⓓ   40. Ⓐ Ⓑ Ⓒ Ⓓ
13. Open-response   27. Ⓐ Ⓑ Ⓒ Ⓓ   41. Open-response
14. Short-answer   28. Ⓐ Ⓑ Ⓒ Ⓓ   42. Open-response

Completely darken bubbles with a No. 2 pencil. If you make a mistake, be sure to erase mark completely. Erase all stray marks.

1. YOUR NAME: _____

(Print) Last First M.I.

SIGNATURE: _____ **DATE:** __/__/__

HOME ADDRESS: _____
(Print) Number

_____
City State Zip Code

PHONE NO.: _____
(Print)

5. YOUR NAME

First 4 letters of last name				FIRST INIT	MID INIT

A B C D E F G H I J K L M N O P Q R S T U V W X Y Z

IMPORTANT: Please fill in these boxes exactly as shown on the back cover of your test book.

2. TEST FORM

3. TEST CODE

4. REGISTRATION NUMBER

6. DATE OF BIRTH

Month	Day	Year
JAN		
FEB		
MAR	0 0	0 0
APR	1 1	1 1
MAY	2 2	2 2
JUN	3 3	3 3
JUL	4 4	4
AUG	5 5	5
SEP	7 7	7
OCT	8 8	8
NOV	9 9	9
DEC		

Test code bubbles: 0 A, 1 B, 2 C, 3 D, 4 E, 5 F, 7 G, 8, 9 (with numeric columns 0-9)

7. SEX
MALE FEMALE

The Princeton Review
© 1996 Princeton Review L.L.C.
FORM NO. 00001-PR

Practice Test ②

1. A B C D
2. A B C D
3. A B C D
4. A B C D
5. A B C D
6. A B C D
7. A B C D
8. A B C D
9. A B C D
10. A B C D
11. Short-answer
12. Short-answer
13. Open-response
14. Short-answer
15. Short-answer
16. Open-response
17. A B C D
18. A B C D
19. A B C D
20. A B C D
21. Open-response
22. Open-response
23. A B C D
24. A B C D
25. A B C D
26. A B C D
27. A B C D
28. A B C D
29. A B C D
30. A B C D
31. A B C D
32. A B C D
33. A B C D
34. A B C D
35. A B C D
36. A B C D
37. A B C D
38. A B C D
39. A B C D
40. A B C D
41. Open-response
42. Open-response

About the Author

Jeff Rubenstein is the Assistant Vice President of Research and Development for K–12 programs at The Princeton Review. He is the author of several books and articles on test preparation.